# FRED HENDERSON

## BREAKDOWN DOCTOR

READING ROOM PUBLISHING

Copyright © 2005 Fred Henderson

First edition published in 2005 by Reading Room Publishing,
45, Forest Road, Warsop, Mansfield, Nottinghamshire,
England, NG20 0ER

Fred Henderson asserts the moral rights to
be identified as the author of this work.

All rights reserved; no part of this publication may be reproduced, stored in a retrieval system, or transmitted in any form or by any recording, or otherwise without the prior written permission of the Publisher, nor be otherwise circulated in any form of binding or cover other than that in which it is published and without similar condition being imposed on the subsequent purchaser.

ISBN 0-9548056-2-3

Printed and Bound by Robinson Media
Ilkeston
Derbyshire

Cover illustration by Mary Birchenall

*God put me on this earth to carry out a number of tasks. At the present time I am so far behind I will probably never be allowed to die.*

Fred Henderson

# Acknowledgements

Spending an entire lifetime working in one's chosen profession, then deciding to write a book about a certain segment of it made me realise the many debts I owe to people who gave me help, guidance and encouragement. It also made me appreciate the information and know-how I gleaned from many of them. The hesitation with which I approach the duty of thanking them is caused by doubts as to my ability to do so adequately; certain that I should have forgotten someone to whom thanks were due and uncertain of the order in which I should mention those that I have remembered.

I am grateful for having been born on a farm and being brought up by such an independent and loving family. I'm sure I must have inherited my determination and love of hard work from my mother who always felt she took things easy if she hadn't worked an 18-hour day and this was every day, 365 days a year. I am forever grateful to neighbouring farmer Frank Jackson who completely restored my confidence and got me 'bump started' after I had been so ill. He used to give me things to do and leave me to do them, jobs that I would never have dreamt of contemplating, never mind completing. However, I suppose it was my time with Alan Bromley that really shaped my future and I hope Dorothy, his widow, will have happy memories when she reads these chapters. So far as this book is concerned my biggest debt of gratitude is to Alan Able of Ansa Motors who had the good foresight to employ me and it was while working for Alan that my experiences of life became so broad. The many stories and experiences, which I recount, were while I was in his employ. I took so much knowledge from him which has stood me in good stead ever since.

The core of my present business is still based on practices that were gleaned during my time with him. During this time I have been married to Valerie (always affectionately known as Joyce) for 34 years and we had two wonderful sons, Jon and David. All three have had to take second place to cars and breakdowns. While each of these people has made a more than significant contribution to my life, the person who made the greatest contribution to this book is Shirley Waldock. She fully expected to retire to the City of Durham to continue her study of Romans only to find a new life in encouraging me to produce this book. I am therefore indebted to her for the hundreds of hours that she has spent helping and researching. Without her my life would have been no different but this book would not have happened.

## Copyright Acknowledgements

Road Rescue Recovery Association for permission to replicate the cover photograph of John Carnivale's Diamond T (Highway Recovery A1 Ltd.)

The British Library for permission to publish photographs previously featured in the Durham Advertiser.

Reasonable attempts have been made to contact all copyright owners of other material used in this book.

# Foreword

My first meeting with Fred Henderson gave no hint that it would change my life for ever. As it turned out, it decided my career, provided my lifelong hobby and, most important of all, resulted in a friendship which has so far lasted almost 40 years.

Fred walked into the city centre offices of the Durham Advertiser, where I was serving a six-year apprenticeship as a journalist. He asked for a reporter to cover Durham Automobile Club's premier event, a road rally called the Dales. Because I had just been convicted of speeding, the news editor decided that I was the man for the job.

Until then, a motor car was just something to get me from A to B, and motor sport was virtually unknown to me. On that Dales Rally, Fred arranged for me to sit in the passenger seat of the course car (which ran ahead of the competitors, to make sure that all the control points were where they should be). I was violently sick, but I was hooked.

Within a few months, I became a regular competitor myself, although it only required a few wooden spoons in autotests and hill climbs to convince me that I was a better navigator than I would ever be a driver.

My own lack of talent behind the wheel was confirmed all too thoroughly by a major accident near Durham (for the benefit of those who know the area, the spot is appropriately named Pity Me), wrecking my Mini and putting me in hospital for six months. During my enforced rest, much of it in traction, Fred was a tower of strength, sorting out all the annoying problems, which would normally fall to one's family (mine were living in Beirut, so bedside visits were none too practical).

Once I was back on my feet, Fred persuaded me that - as a professional journalist - I should take over editorship of the motor club magazine. There was no desktop publishing in those days: I wrote the copy and did the layouts, while Fred actually produced the magazine on a hand-driven printer.

To satisfy the ego of our club members (and ourselves, of course) we used to send a copy of each month's magazine to all the UK's 'real' magazines that covered motor sport. This may or may not have raised the profile of Durham Automobile Club, but it did lead directly to my being offered a job on Cars & Car Conversions magazine, since when I have been lucky enough to work full-time in motor sport, going on to edit Rally Sport and Motor Racing magazines before becoming press officer for the RAC Rally, the British Grand Prix and, eventually, the World Rally Championship.

Until Cars & Car Conversions took me away from Durham, however, I spent much of my spare time with Fred. There was motor club business to be transacted, of course, but I also enjoyed riding out with him on breakdown calls. His ability to analyse and repair almost any mechanical or electrical problem at the roadside was (and still is) quite remarkable. I have known him to correctly diagnose a problem by asking the stranded motorist to run the engine while Fred listened on the telephone!

These activities, mainly nocturnal and often in foul weather (that's when cars break down, after all) showed me what smooth driving really was, which impression was reinforced when I myself ended up beside Fred on many, many rallies. He was a navigator's dream driver, able to maintain a surprisingly fast, but absolutely safe pace for days on end. International rallies in those days lasted up to five days and it was quite normal to drive 36 hours with no real rest. Fred would be running at the same pace on day five as he had on day one, with the same lack of mistakes. He also hated not to finish an event, and would nurse cars to the end with no suspension, no lights, or missing several gears.

From time to time, sometimes to fight back from adversity, or at the request of a sponsor, Fred would drive at 100%, showing sheer speed which could easily have taken him into the ranks of professional rally drivers, if he had cared to devote the required time and effort. Fred, however, has always known what he wanted from life: his family, his home and his thriving breakdown business (maybe also his cricket!) are far more important than mere motor sport. Quite right, too.

Colin Wilson

# CHAPTER I

It was just after twenty past eight on a cold and wet February morning as I stood in a back yard adjoining an old disused stable, secured by two double doors and what appeared at the time to be an enormous padlock. I was preparing to start a new job as an apprentice motor mechanic in what could only be described as a back street garage in Willington, some 10 miles west of Durham City. As I stood there, more in apprehension than excitement, I couldn't even remember what time I was due to start work. By now I had realised, since the place was still locked up, that it obviously wasn't 8 o'clock and I couldn't honestly remember whether I should be starting at half past eight or 9 o'clock. As it got to quarter to nine, I even wondered whether I was there on the right day.

Not being the most confident of people I would only speak when spoken to providing I was answering a question, because that was the easiest way to speak. I was almost six feet tall, painfully shy and weighing just about 9 stone with wrists the same thickness as a standard broom shank and ankles that looked as if they had trouble supporting me. They often came into view rather easily as I had grown so fast in the last few months that it was impossible to get trousers that were always long enough in the leg. While my confidence in dealing with people was non-existent, my confidence in most other aspects of life was bubbling over. I'd been born and brought up on a mixed dairy farm of less than 100 acres. My whole world and I suppose that of my sister Margaret who was three years my junior had revolved around agriculture. Both my parents' connection with farming went back several generations and I didn't have a blood relative who was not involved in farming. My parents had endured a hard working life with little luxury including for many years no electricity, but nothing would stop them. They talked fondly about the winter of 1947 when the farm was completely isolated for six weeks with not even a radio for communication after the accumulator went flat in the first week. As the years unfolded I would develop the skills and determination and the sheer doggedness that must have been present during those six weeks. In any case it was now about to be put to the test.

The garage was run by a self-employed motor mechanic called Alan Bromley who, with no energy wasted on imagination, traded as 'Bromley's Garage'. At least people knew who and what they were dealing with, which was a vital ingredient in a still thriving mining community. It was impossible to forget that it was a mining community because the whole of Willington was over-shadowed by the most enormous slagheap that I have ever seen. This pit heap must have been 200 feet high and covered more than 20 acres. The garage, which was to become work to me for the next five years, was situated just a few hundred yards from the base of this huge slag pile. This unwanted landmark was the legacy of over a hundred years of waste from the nearby mine, ineptly-named Brancepeth Colliery, which was an insult to a picturesque village some three miles away with no industry at all let alone one as dirty and grimy as the workings named after it. The slagheap stood silent and still, apart from the clanking of some machine dropping yet another load from the bowels of the earth. Living and working nearby was not so tranquil when the hot summer months came and the stiff wind whipped the razor sharp dust across the whole of the town, including the secluded back yard of our workshop. The eyesore was to make a hasty exit several years later following the landslip at Aberfan, South Wales in 1966, which claimed the lives of many. Where it went or how it went I never did find out, but one day, long after I had left Bromley's Garage, the slagheap and all the dust was gone.

Just after 9 o'clock I was alerted by the arrival of a Land Rover, hastily parked, and out jumped my employer to be, Alan. I had met him some 10 days earlier during the course of my rather informal interview, when I had stood at the side of the vehicle that Alan was working on as he beavered away with his head under the bonnet. No CV, no references, just a few words exchanged. I was pleasantly surprised that he still remembered who I was.

Alan brought out an enormous bunch of keys and slotted the right key straight into the lock and swinging open the doors he asked me if I would drive a couple of cars out. I hesitated, though to be quite honest, even though I had only ventured on to the public roads with a David Brown tractor complete with a range of appropriate implements, I felt I was a better driver than he was. I'd been ploughing a straight furrow for the last five or six years but had to remember I was still under age for driving a motor vehicle on the roads and I wasn't sure if a stable yard in a town was public highway. So, after a series of grunts, Alan quickly reversed out the vehicles that would start and we pushed out two others that wouldn't fire up. He didn't seem at all bothered by my presence and I started to wonder whether I'd come to a proper job.

It transpired that the business had been running for about four years and in all that time I was the first person Alan had employed. I was 15 and had been brought up on a small dairy farm with very little contact with the outside world so it felt really strange to be in a town and in an environment where I was obviously going to come into contact with people. I was to struggle with this for the next 20 years because prior to working for Alan I had a desire only to work on the farm and to be involved with mechanical things.

This was not my first choice of occupation. I had always hoped to be an agricultural engineer working on tractors and farm machinery. My father had tried to get my name down at the only local Agent, J.G. Paxton & Sons who had been trading since 1860, but he had not been successful. This was probably because he hadn't bought enough new tractors: in fact, he hadn't bought any in recent years. All the Agricultural Agent would say was, "If we need any help, we'll send for you." It was always in the back of my mind, year after year, how things might have worked out. I always remembered what had been said, even after some 30 years when one of their vans came to my premises and the driver asked for me, I thought, "Good God, not after all this time!" Then I realised the driver was not even born when I had been trying to get a job like his.

Nevertheless, I thought that sooner or later I was going to have to do something or other, but obviously it had never entered any of my thoughts that it might be a good idea to ask. It was not long before I was told to break up a wooden box and get a bucketful of coke from outside the workshop in order to get the stove going. The stove was a round, pot-bellied cylinder with a lid on the top and a hole at the bottom to clean out the clinker, like something from 'The Great Escape'. The fire was there to take the chill off the premises and get rid of the cloying dampness that had gathered over the course of the previous weekend. As Alan started to throw wood into the top of the stove, together with various quantities of anything that would burn, like petrol and thinners, he told me to watch myself as he threw in a match. There was a fairly resounding thud, I'm sure the cast iron stove seemed to expand, then contract as the whole thing lit up. Alan threw in half a bucketful of coke, shut the lid and said, "That'll be alright by 10 o'clock." I eventually mastered the technique for lighting this contraption but not before I had lost two sets of eyebrows in the process. Apart from being the main focal point, the stove served many other purposes; it would heat a pie or a tin of beans with no effort and was also used to rid the place of rubbish. When it was going well and glowing cherry red the pot-bellied monstrosity would burn anything including finger ends.

I began to survey my surroundings and was thankful that it obviously had been a stable because it felt just a bit like home on the farm. Not only was the floor still cobbled it also featured a slight slope and a drainage channel. The gaps between the cobbles had started to fill up with a combination of dirt and old oil, making it just about level enough to work with a jack and axle stands. We certainly had no ramps or lifting equipment because the total headroom was little more than eight feet which, my grandfather assured me, was about the right height for a stable as this helped to keep the horses warm in extreme weather.

A wooden bench made from railway sleepers was fitted at one end, the same end as the stove, and the whole place was lit with four small strip lights. Above the main workshop was the former granary that was accessed, in true agricultural style, by a stone staircase just like on my father's farm. The granary had been converted to a really useful and organised store where a remarkable range of spare parts was kept.

The granary area was three times the size of the workshop because it also stretched over a lock-up garage that was occupied by somebody else. A telephone was placed on a small wooden desk in the stores area adjacent to a large comfortable armchair which Alan claimed had been dumped in his yard. He didn't waste anything, another lesson I have never forgotten. Little did I realise, as I wandered about trying not to look out of place, what a profound effect working in these premises was to have on almost every aspect of what I was to do in years to come.

The garage was no more than four miles from home. In order to get to work I had to cycle the one mile from the farm to where I could catch a bus to Willington. I was always pleased that the road to the bus stop was downhill because time was always of the essence in the morning. The reverse would be true of my return journey when the uphill gradient felt like the last resort after a long day. On my way to the village bus stop I had to bounce over the railway level crossing. If I turned right and had been able to cycle along the railway tracks I would have arrived at work on a route almost as the crow flies. Everyone used to say to me, "Why don't you use the train?" It was not easy to explain and normally I didn't even try, but I had already developed a problem about travelling on a train which had started when I was no more than six years old.

My route to school was to leave the house at two minutes to eight and toddle the one mile to the railway station, watched carefully for the first half-mile by my mum to ensure that I didn't stop off to play with wild rabbits and things. On arrival at the station I would form up with four or five other pupils. The oldest, who was probably about 14, made sure that we all got on and off the train safely. However, because there was a measles or mumps epidemic on this particular day, I was the only pupil travelling. I was fairly unmoved by the whole occasion, handing over my tuppence and being issued with a little cardboard ticket which was duly stamped in a heavy metal machine to confirm I was fit and ready to embark on my journey. The time now was about half past eight in the morning and the journey to school would take no more than two minutes. The train was of the rural variety with a small steam engine in the front and four or five individual carriages with separate compartments that were not linked to each other. When the train arrived the Station Master opened the carriage door just behind the engine, tapped me on the head and grunted, shutting the door safely behind me. As I had been travelling the route for the best part of a year, I knew exactly what was coming and where to get off, or where I hoped to get off. I didn't have a care in the world until, as the train drew to a standstill, it suddenly dawned on me.

For whatever reason, railway carriage doors of that era did not have an inside handle, the intention being to release a large strap and buckle arrangement which would then lower the window, allowing the passenger to reach outside and open the door. I now realised that I had two or three problems. I was hardly tall enough to see out of the window so no one could see me struggling and at the age of six I had nowhere near the strength that London North Eastern Railways had anticipated should be used to release the window. Even if I could manage to open the window, I was far too short in the arm and leg to reach the handle. To make matters worse the whole scene was covered by steam and smoke from the locomotive that was just ahead of me. So, before anyone realised what was happening, I was on the move again.

Now, this was new. I had never been this way before and panic started to set in. Would I ever be found? What would happen to me? In the next 10 minutes we called at two more small stations with the same result, I could not attract any attention nor could I get the window down. In a short while we stopped again but this time there was no platform and no people. After what seemed to be a lifetime, but was probably 15 or 20 minutes during which time, I later found out, the engine had been taking on water; we set off on a seemingly never-ending journey which eventually ended in some railway sidings in Sunderland. Then everything went quiet and I was left trapped and cornered. All I could see out of the window was other railway carriages that looked as if they had been there for years. I was sure I would have to die, not only that, my remains wouldn't be found for years. It was only the second time out for my new school cap, what a waste of money that had been. Then, after what were probably only a few hours, some people arrived to clean the carriages. They set about their work expecting to find the usual old piecrusts and cigarette ends. Imagine their surprise when they came across a child.

At this stage the full 1950s emergency services went into action. I was questioned as to how I had got there and where I had come from. They quickly realised I was not squatting so I was taken to the nearest signal box for a meeting with two men in Station Masters' uniforms who quickly decided that I needed to be repatriated to Brandon School some 20 miles back. After a few timetables were scanned, they realised that a coke train was about to leave to go to Willington, which meant I could be dropped off at school. To make sure I didn't get up to any mischief they placed me in the Guard's Van, a fairly luxurious hut towed behind the train. It had a marvellous coke stove and a friendly guard who insisted I had one of his egg sandwiches and some of his tea, which he had just made, courtesy of the coke stove. I really enjoyed that trip back to school.

With a lot of skill and calculation the engine towing this huge snake drew to a halt some distance past Brandon Station but just precise enough to allow the guard's van to be in the centre of the platform. I was handed over to the Brandon Station Master who suggested I nip off to school before I was missed. It was now one minute after half past three so as I approached the school I was met by pupils finishing their lessons for the day and by a teacher who asked where I had been. When I explained the story she insisted on us going back to the station so she could hear it for herself. As she finished the brief discussion with the Station Master she reminded me that in 10 minutes time my train for Brancepeth would arrive. Without saying a word, in case it was the wrong one, I ran out of the station and made a bee-line for home, which involved getting out of the small built-up area and into the countryside which, even at that age, I knew very well. I had to climb several fences and hedges and go through fields with cattle and sheep and over one field that had been recently ploughed. As I arrived home, on time for what would have been a normal day, I wondered how I would explain all this to my mum and dad especially as I would probably need a sick note to account for my absence from school. I didn't have to worry because the teacher who had seen me run away had gone back to the school and together with the headmaster had driven to the farm to see if I was all right or probably to report that I had gone missing in Brandon.

I cannot remember more than the discussion taking something like 30 seconds and the whole thing was dismissed as damned unfortunate and tomorrow everyone would make certain that I got out of the train at Brandon; which they duly did. In fact, for the next few months the train was not allowed to leave the station before it was established that there were no trapped school children on board.

On a day-to-day basis the whole episode made no difference to me but for at least 10 years, once on a train, I was never happy until I'd got off it. By the age of seven I'd abandoned the train and converted to the bus, which meant a further quarter of a mile walk at both ends, but I felt much safer and this feeling of safety was paramount in my decision, at the ripe old age of 15, to use the bus as the preferred option.

Nowadays I never understand why I didn't just cycle the whole distance particularly as I was a competent cyclist by necessity. After all, I had covered a thousand miles a year cycling around Brancepeth. All this was achieved riding a Triumph Palm Beach Tourer complete with Sturmey Archer three-speed gears and a tyre-driven dynamo for those nights when the moon wasn't out. This machine was a present for my eleventh birthday and was still going strong five years and 5,000 miles later. Eventually it was left to rust in peace, giving way to a vehicle with an engine.

It was not long before my working role became clearly defined. Not only did I work as an apprentice motor mechanic, a job I found extremely easy to do and thoroughly enjoyable, I was also expected to complete what seemed to be a never-ending list of chores. These ranged from lighting the fire on a morning to putting the cars in at night and throwing out the rubbish. In between I went backwards and forwards to the shop, up and down the street for other bits and pieces, painted the walls when there was no work and even learned how to answer the telephone. This came about when it continued to ring and I discovered that Alan, during the long drawn out process of selling one of his second-hand cars, had disappeared into the nearby pub.

How this licensed establishment ever made a living defeated me. It only ever had one or two retired miners and their 'marras' propping up the bar and having the odd game of darts or dominoes. The place was run by lady called Maud who, to give her the benefit of the doubt, was probably in her late 30s and with dark hair that suggested she would have been very attractive in her younger days. But she was loud and verbally aggressive if any of her clientele caused problems, usually because she'd sold them too much alcohol. Quite often Maud would have a go at Alan or me about parked cars and while Alan would stand up to her I would just get out of the way. This was because I didn't have the ability to construct any serious discussion or argument. Even when I was old enough to enter licensed premises, pubs just didn't appeal to me, I always thought they were better viewed from the outside.

While this was a definite functional garage with an outstanding reputation, the facilities were almost non-existent. There was one tap-cum-hosepipe; if you wanted to fill the cooling system on a car you stuck it in the top of the radiator, if it was for a mug of tea you stuck it in the kettle, which was boiled on a gas ring connected by a piece of petrol pipe to a gas pipe sticking out of the floor. There was no meter or tap so whoever paid for the gas was anyone's guess. One day, when the flame was low, we decided to clean the pipe by giving it a blowback with the airline, subjecting the gas main to 150 pounds per square inch in the wrong direction. We probably blew out half the pilot lights in Willington. It took three days for the gas to return, still with no pressure. Not to be defeated, the kettle boiled just as well on the stove.

I once, and only once, asked about the toilet and was told, "Half way up the street beside the bus stop." I later found it best not to go on the quarter-hour as it would be full of passengers dropped off by the local bus. Part of my streetwise training told me not to use a warm seat and to keep clear if the chain was still swinging. The left-hand cubicle confused me as someone had stolen not only the chain but also part of the seat.

We did have further assistance, to use the word loosely, in the form of a well-retired miner called Wilf who would wander in and make the tea, which meant it was one less job for me to do. I always recall Wilf with a certain amount of fondness as he was totally misplaced in a repair garage but appeared to enjoy in-depth conversations with Alan, the contents of which I never understood then or now. Wilf had the most peculiar shade of white false teeth and he always claimed to keep them decent by putting them in a jar of Domestos overnight which, over a number of years, had done the enamel no good at all. It came as no surprise that, after knowing him for only a few years, he died of some stomach complaint. The odd person did remark that it might have been his teeth that killed him. The big problem with Wilf dying meant that I had to make the tea again, morning, noon and night. However, I felt the full benefit of promotion as I was given Wilf's keys, which meant not having to hang about in the cold whilst waiting for someone to open up each morning.

By the end of the first year I had developed my natural flair to a good level and was able to undertake repair work that would normally be associated with more experienced mechanics. Alan entrusted me to look after the business, not only while he was out buying and selling cars, but also when he went on annual holiday to Redcar from where he would return twice during the week in case there was money in the till.

I found the role of being in charge particularly daunting. When I had to deal with customers they never seemed straightforward and were reluctant to take my word seriously. I had a slight advantage when conducting business on the telephone because the customers were not able to see how naïve I was. Thank goodness the customer-base didn't include female customers of the younger variety or I would have been at sixes and sevens. It was more usual for me to have the typical battleaxe to sort out. Because I was not old enough to drive on the road I had to arrange for any distant spare parts to be sent on the bus as an unaccompanied parcel, something the bus companies were pleased to do in those days. On an odd occasion I even had to travel on the bus myself to pick up parts.

As an appreciation for my efforts my wages, before off-takes, had been increased to £3.10s for a 44-hour week. This was a substantial increase from the £2.12.6d I was paid when I first started the job. The extra 17/6d (82p today) made such a difference to my life-style, as I was now able to afford to go to the Durham Town Hall dance on a Saturday night. Friends of mine said, "You couldn't go there unless you were prepared to get rid of 10 shillings." I found that I could have a really good night and not even spend anything like that amount of money. The biggest expense was getting into the dance hall, which featured a live multi-piece band with a girl singer. This cost me 3 shillings and with export beer at 1/9d a bottle, even allowing for buying one other person a drink, I still finished up with change from my original 10-bob note (50p today).

I am reminded of some of the other costs that used to eat into a weekly wage. A chicken and stuffing sandwich would get rid of 3d (just over 1/2p) and petrol was 4/6d (22p) a gallon. If I'd been a fully skilled mechanic I would have been entitled to a wage of £10 or £11 per week, but on such high earnings would have suffered the penalty of having to pay income tax.

Whilst my usual working day was from 8.30 a.m. until 5.30 p.m., I would often work until nine or ten o'clock at night during the summer months. I would be persuaded into such actions by the opportunity to tackle more varied and interesting jobs. For example, replacing burnt valves in a cylinder head and hearing the finished vehicle running so much better gave a good sense of job satisfaction. One of the main advantages of working in the summer was that many jobs could be done outside in the yard. I have to say that during some of the long hot summers that we experienced in those days, my working conditions were considerably better than those of many of the other apprentice motor mechanics that I came into contact with when I started night school at the local Technical College. This academic side of the job was something that had to be tackled two nights a week and went on for a period of four years.

On one summer day, while fitting a clutch to an Austin A55 estate car, which was one of very few cars to be equipped with a radio, we gathered round in earnest to hear the blow-by-blow account as Alan Shepard became the first American to blast off into space. Some time later we listened with just as much enthusiasm when John Glenn completed a full "lap" of the earth.

A passing interest in the Space Programme led to an old transistor radio appearing in the workshop. It was not quite as easy to find anything else to listen to, especially with my peculiar tastes. The general opinion was that we should be switched to the Home Service, which was for people of a higher intellect, but that was too much for me; I preferred to twiddle until I found the Light Programme, even if I had to endure 'Listen with Mother' and 'Woman's Hour'. However, Saturday mornings were quite good and 'Saturday Club' with Brian Matthews was a real chance to hear popular music. If I had to choose one single year in a life that was best for good records, it would be 1962. It was the start of the Liverpool revolution and there were so many good solo artists. One of these was Susan Maughan who lived at nearby Consett but I could not have cared if she had lived in the Outer Hebrides, she had such a nice voice and the song 'Bobby's Girl' was absolutely wonderful.

During my time at Bromley's garage I certainly learned about customer loyalty. Every action in this tight knit business community seemed to be affected by a further action based on a form of loyalty that Alan referred to as: "You scratch my back and I'll scratch yours." Any departure from this approach could have serious consequences. For example, at 10 o'clock each morning I was dispatched along the High Street to pick up chicken sandwiches from the local butcher's shop. Then, one morning, without explanation I was ordered to go to the baker's shop higher up the street. It turned out that the butcher had bought a van from some other garage and his chicken sandwiches had suddenly made Alan ill. It was only a few months later that the baker decided to buy a new Morris 1100, so he was another local businessman who fell out of the food chain. Within six months I was down to the last port of call for our morning break. I had gone from chicken sandwiches to meat pies and was now on Cornish pasties whether I liked it or not.

Food was not the only thing that was subject to this regime. Alan discovered I'd been in a pub in Willington where the landlord was not a customer and I was strongly advised to patronise a spit-and-sawdust place at the other end of town. This was not because the beer or company was any better but because the landlord had two vehicles that he sent to us for regular service and repairs. I was also told which barber should cut my hair. This caused me some confusion as he was a non-driver and went around on a pedal cycle, which at that time we didn't work on. So there must have been some other reason. I was strongly advised to change doctors because the practice I attended had all their vehicles maintained elsewhere. This was something I refused to do. The nonsense never seemed to go away. I had been talking to Alan about buying my first real suit. The next thing I knew a customer with a tailoring business was virtually measuring me up. Even when I was busy checking for a noisy tappet Alan attempted to influence the style and design of my new suit. Probably he and the customer were sizing up the opportunity to get rid of some old cloth.

The final crunch came after three days of excruciating toothache from a rear molar that had been well destroyed by my liking for Fry's Chocolate Crème. Alan suggested I visit a dentist who not only presented his Riley Pathfinder for regular service with us but his wife also used a Triumph Herald. Alan led me to believe that after a couple of injections the tooth would be removed and I could return to work and finish off an exhaust repair on a Standard Vanguard. How wrong he was. I took off my overalls, left the garage and walked into the dentist's surgery where I asked for the offending tooth to be removed.

I remember wondering what the strange smell was. Later I discovered it was stale whisky.

Over the next 10 or 15 minutes I thought I was going to die as the whisky sodden dentist reached for implement after implement to finally get my tooth clear. I think he finally succeeded by selecting a pair of parrot nose pliers similar to the ones I would use to break off a rusty hose clip. Emerging from the surgery covered in blood, I knew I had to get home. I jumped on to the nearest passing bus and the conductor was so disturbed by my appearance that he didn't even charge me the fare. As I stumbled from the bus I was still faced with a mile and a half walk to the farm. I was lucky because the first vehicle to come along stopped because the driver thought I'd had an accident. He took me straight home. It was four days before I could return to work, by which time the Vanguard was long gone. From then on it became my decision where I would go for my pies, beer, clothes and more importantly which dentist I would use.

It was three years later when the magnitude of this horrible experience became apparent. I had attended my family dentist for a check up and was told three of my teeth had to come out. Memories of my previous visit to the dentist came flooding back; I convinced myself that this situation would be three times as bad. I booked a week's holiday and had my father drive me to the surgery. However, the job was done with such a different level of skill that I could have gone back to work that afternoon, so I had wasted some holiday. Even so, this whole episode is something that remains etched forever on my jaw. These later extractions left a smooth finish, whereas on the other side of my mouth the tooth removed by the Riley Pathfinder dentist had left a permanent 'trench' in my jawbone.

Using my pedal cycle with three-speed gears and dynamo, combined with the number 42 bus and timetabling permitting, meant the journey from home to work was around 45 minutes in each direction. This resulted in a loss of almost one and a half hours each day in travelling time. I decided, much against my parents' wishes, to look for some sort of motorbike. Eventually, when one duly appeared for the vast sum of £10 (4 weeks' wages), I embarked on a career as a motorcyclist. The machine was not actually a motorbike but a very old 125cc Vespa scooter. After one or two brief journeys to and from work, mechanical unreliability began to set in and I spent more time pushing than riding. It eventually dawned on me why it was only ten pounds – I'd been robbed even at that price! But I couldn't escape from the time saving factor and persuaded my father to invest in a better machine. He could see the advantage of me being home earlier in the evening to help on the farm.

This newer deluxe model was a BSA 250cc Sunbeam scooter equipped with a twin-cylinder four-stroke engine delivering smooth power at all times and proved incredibly reliable. A scooter with this sort of power was unusual and some people thought I might finish up in a heap at the side of the road. Like my old push bike, the Sunbeam was only used out of necessity and when the snow reached six or seven inches in depth, I had to find other ways of getting to work. I was still underage to drive a car on the road but everyone had accepted that my scooter was probably not as dangerous as had been suggested.

However, opinions were about to change. One Friday evening I filled my donkey jacket pockets with a recently tinned soldering iron, a couple of screwdrivers and a spool of wire. I then set off for the village Youth Club where I'd been tasked to repair and replace some speakers that led from the gramophone to other parts of the village hall. The narrow tarmac road from the farm involved a couple of dips and blind brows going through a tree line. The wind had been gusting for some time but not enough to challenge a by now relatively experienced motorcyclist. I crested the first blind brow in the tree line and as the single headlight settled back on the road it picked out a large sycamore tree in the process of being blown down by the wind. It was perhaps some 20 yards ahead, which was all the distance the light would reach. The tree was falling slowly so I felt I had time to go underneath it. This proved to be a poor assumption as the tree fell to the ground. The main trunk was about two feet in diameter; its branches were sticking out everywhere. I was perhaps travelling too fast, as we all do at that age and slithered into the foliage and branches at what seemed unabated speed. The Sunbeam stopped abruptly and I was catapulted over the tree, landing on the road some distance ahead.

    I landed on my head and as I came round in the pitch darkness a man and a woman were talking to me. Beside them was a Morris 1000 van. As my eyes came into focus I noticed I was about two feet from the front wheel. After establishing who I was, and realising I wasn't dead, they bundled me into the back of their van and took me home. I must have blacked out because I still can't recall what must have been a six-mile detour as the road was completely blocked by the fallen sycamore. I was very grateful to be back home and my father and mother came to help me from the van to the house. My injuries couldn't have been too bad as I clearly recall seeing a black and white television in the corner of the living room showing a programme starring Dennis Weaver as McCloud with the famous catch phrase of 'Coming Mr. Dillon.' There then followed a discussion as to whether a doctor should be called or whether I should be simply fed a cup of tea with plenty of sugar in case I was in shock.

Eventually the doctor was telephoned who arranged for an ambulance to take me off to hospital. After being stuck on a trolley forever (not much different from today) I was finally diagnosed as suffering from a badly broken nose and a hairline fracture at the rear of my skull. Because of this I was kept in hospital for a week, which I felt was a bit unnecessary. I must have taken quite a bang on the head because it was some weeks after discharge from hospital before I could completely recall the accident. In the meantime, my father had gone with the tractor and trailer to recover my scooter, which had suffered remarkably little damage. Much to my disgust I was made to stay off work for four weeks, which gave me enough time to search the area where I was able to recover my recently tinned soldering iron and my parrot nose pliers from the nearby hedgerow. After this incident I didn't have much enthusiasm for two wheels but continued for another six months until I was able to take over my grandfather's car.

While the summers of '61 and '62 were fantastic I also had to endure in my unique working environment the surprisingly cold winter of 1963. What started as a fall of snow and a sharp frost continued from January right through to March. Every day was high drama in just getting to and from work in the constant cold and the never-ending flurries of snow. By the time the thaw had set in, the yard at the back of the workshop was covered in three feet of ice. For six weeks we'd been working three feet off the ground.

When not working as an apprentice motor mechanic at the garage, my spare time was taken up working on my father's farm and on another large farm nearby. Frank Jackson, who ran this large mixed farm, always had enormous confidence in my ability to handle farm machinery. Our friendship goes back to when I was only 12 years old when he would collect me after tea and sit me on a tractor. He would then deliver me back home in time to go to bed. On leaving school and waiting to start work at a local agricultural engineers (a job that never materialised) I spent my time working on Frank's farm. I always think of what a great debt I owe to him. He was able to get me involved in a vast array of farm machinery that I would never have experienced at home on our small dairy farm. This doubtless led to my driving skills being exposed and developed from a remarkably early age.

I don't ever remember feeling tired or fed up but just looked forward to the next interesting thing. Perhaps whilst ploughing a field on a Sunday I would be thinking about a cylinder head gasket to be fitted to a Morris 1000 on Monday morning. If the day dragged in the workshop I would look forward to driving some farm machinery while my father went for his tea that evening.

I often recall how I came to hate school and most of the pupils, including girls, who would bully me. I had lost a lot of schooling due to illness and this put me behind with schoolwork. Combined with dyslexia, a condition not then recognised, I was a prime target for school playground bullying. During my months of illness I was not always confined to bed and living on a farm there was plenty of fresh air outside and with an inventive mind and a great curiosity I spent some of my time making working scale-models or pursuing and observing the natural world around me. While it is something I have never extended to later life, I was then very curious as to how some species of wildlife functioned.

I once got the idea of coating a bumblebee with flour and then tracking it back to where it disappeared down a hole in the ground. I went back and got a spade and followed the hole which was only a couple of inches underground until I came to the bumblebee's nest. Knowing that these creatures are not particularly vicious I then went back after the hours of darkness, popped the whole lot into an old one-gallon paint tin with a hole in the bottom, just like a miniature hive. I finished up with 12 bumblebee hives at the rear of one of the farm buildings. I watched in wonderment as the cycle of life evolved; how the tins gave off one or two queen bumblebees and how in subsequent years these developed their own little colonies in nearby brick cavities and other little alcoves around the farm. Descendants of these little creatures were still milling about some years later, which proved that in the wild they obviously didn't travel far each year. Mechanical challenges were always foremost on my mind. I remember building a windmill that drove a dynamo that, in turn, would charge a battery to power the family wireless.

One October when some of the horrible little bullying brats were potato picking I, yes, little me, was driving the machine that removed the potatoes from the ground and spread them over a 6ft area to make them easy to collect and put into sacks. As I passed one of the pickers, Bernard, whom I particularly disliked, I simply speeded up the tractor and the crop that he was responsible for collecting went 10 yards further on across the field. I knew then that I had learned a valuable lesson that the chance to get even will come sooner or later but will always come if you wait.

My feelings of resentment towards this school bullying never left me. Twenty-five years later when this Bernard character came into my business saying his vehicle had broken down nearby and would I offer assistance, he was completely taken aback when I refused any form of help. I reminded him of what he was like and dispatched him from the premises. He left without comment and I felt completely justified that I had started to get my own back.

I had previously managed to get through a motor cycle driving test but one of the main reasons that a motor cycle test was easier to pass was that you were able to stick 'L' plates on and go out and practice and practice: you didn't need to cajole someone to sit with you. So when my 17th birthday arrived in February 1962 my desire to get on to the road was thwarted. My grandfather certainly had no wish for me to drive his Standard Flying 8A and my father mumbled that, in order for me to drive his Morris 16 Cowley, he needed to get me added to his insurance. All this seemed a bit pathetic considering that I had been driving a tractor on country lanes since I was 12, bearing in mind if the local constable had said anything his milk and eggs quota, not to mention his Christmas goose, could have been seriously affected. I eventually persuaded Alan Bromley that Wilf, who was still alive at the time, could accompany me to collect the odd spare part. When he could be bothered, Alan would also take me on the road.

One thing everyone was unanimous about was my driving skills and I had no reason to disagree with them. It was suggested that I should apply for a driving test immediately. Alan said I should take it in the company Land Rover which, according to him, would further demonstrate my skill and promote his business, particularly as the vehicle was sign written with the company name. It came as quite a shock, after taking what I considered to be a perfect test, to be failed on several disciplines. I could only conclude that the people who'd sat with me had never passed a driving test or were so out of date they'd misled me. In many ways I was self-taught. Anyhow, an important lesson had been learned.

I purchased a copy of the Highway Code and then set about doing the job correctly. I had to wait another 28 days before I could take a second test by which time I was prepared to the hilt. I had practiced every question in the Highway Code; I knew every page and every stopping distance. To make certain I didn't miss any road signs I'd ridden my scooter around all the test routes in Durham City. When my test day came I was denied the use of the Land Rover as it was out on a job. The only vehicle available was an old Austin A35 van belonging to a painter and decorator that had been left in for three days' work. We had the presence of mind to remove the ladder from the roof and managed to attach some 'L' plates. I was full of depression to say the least especially when I realised how vicious the clutch was but there was little option, I either had to cancel the test or go ahead with this rickety old van. I chose to go ahead.

On arriving at the Test Centre I was greeted by the examiner. His name was Mr. Purvis who everyone had warned me was the worst examiner in the world. He had an alleged reputation for failing anybody who didn't have firm breasts and a short skirt fitted and I was somewhat shy of these qualifications. In all my life I had never felt so nervous. My future hung on the next three-quarters of an hour. I was dreading the emergency stop in case some of the paint tins finished up in the front. Each time we took a left hand corner something swung in the back and hit the side with a resounding clang, but the dreaded Mr Purvis took everything in his stride. Every statement was plain matter of fact. If he'd only smiled at least once the tension would have eased.

Even though I didn't feel I'd made any mistakes, in the back of my mind I thought he might have spotted an odd error. As we continued I was conscious that I had a lot of tests still to go. The tension mounted as we turned left to go up Red Hills Lane, probably the steepest hill in Durham.

As we approached the gradient Mr Purvis told me to stop half way up and apply the handbrake. I knew what was coming and I knew how the clutch was, but even worse the time was just after four o'clock and the local grammar school was turning out. As I prepared to make my hill start as instructed I suddenly looked to the right and saw a group of Johnson School boys waiting to see what would happen. I mustered every bit of application as I raised the revs on the engine, brought up the clutch and released the handbrake. The clutch pedal began to jump up and down and the vehicle shook awkwardly. So, despite applying the accelerator I gave one mighty lunge and stalled. This brought a loud cheer and a round of applause that must have lasted for ten seconds, at which point Mr Purvis said; "Please make a further hill start." Once again I went through the whole procedure, this time starting with slightly more revs and less time dragging the clutch. The van lunged forward with just a squeal of a rear tyre and the sound of some paint tins rolling towards the back doors. This brought an even bigger round of applause from my appreciative audience.

Feeling that this was the final straw I drove up the rest of the gradient and on to the flat. Surely, all I could do now was go back to the test centre and be failed again. Five minutes later, as we pulled up where we had started at the Test Centre, I was in a terrible mental state when the examiner gave me this piece of pink paper and said: "Congratulations, you have just passed the Driving Test." Then, without further comment, he left the vehicle. I just could not believe it. Having failed so miserably at my first attempt, I was now the proud owner of a full driving license. The lesson learned this time was the more you know about something the less you think you know. Anyway, proverb or no I was on the road after 17 years two months and four days. No matter how many things I look back on as being life-changing or forks in the road of life, passing the driving test was the be-all and end-all and nothing would ever surpass that achievement.

So, finally I was on the road on four wheels but still without the financial resources to buy a vehicle of my own. Occasionally, if I was working late and an old car or van was on site (even if it was unroadworthy) I would be allowed to use it for travelling home. The ulterior motive being that I was sure to be at work on time next day. Some of these vehicles challenged my skills to get them started the next morning; something I never failed to do, defeat would have been unthinkable.

# CHAPTER II

Bromley's Garage was involved in many activities. A main area of work was vehicle breakdown and recovery that was undertaken exclusively by Alan. He would take his old Land Rover home each night in the hope of receiving a call either from the AA or the RAC or, if his luck was really in, the call might be in the form of a road accident.

For someone who did not mind about time of day or day of week, working in this sort of environment started to appeal to me. Usually, I wouldn't get the chance to go with Alan on a breakdown as I had to stay behind and watch the garage, but if I discovered he was going out to another job after hours, I would go along with him in my own time. Even though the number of breakdown jobs was small and the number of road accidents even smaller, I worked hard, honing my skills and hoping one day to get a breakdown or a road accident to do by myself. If Alan was away from the workshop and the phone rang, I would rush up the granary steps praying that it would be a broken down car to be dealt with. Mostly, I was disappointed to find it was someone wanting a puncture repaired in two places.

Following the death of my grandfather, Ernest, I found myself fully mobile. His legacy to me was a much-cherished, though dropping to bits, 1947 Standard Flying 8A. This car was powered by an eight horse-power, side valve engine. It had two forward opening doors that were a terrible fit and a three-speed gearbox with no synchromesh. This meant that gear changing had to be carried out with the utmost precision otherwise a terrible grinding noise would regale everyone in earshot. Six-volt electrics prevailed, which meant that the field of vision at night was almost as good as that of a full moon but at least it was a car and I could now drive to places that had not previously been possible.

While this was far from a quality vehicle I was able to turn up at the local Brancepeth Village Youth Club and as the only car owner, my status went up overnight. As an added bonus some of the girls would now talk to me and a new world was starting to open out. I remember giving a lift to Marion, the prettiest girl in the village (though of course Brancepeth was only a small village) and that she was wearing the most amazing dress that fanned out all over the dashboard. She sat terrified as we rattled along at about 28 mph. As we continued along I noticed that she was in a slightly reclined position because the rear brackets of the front passenger seat had rusted through the floor. It was when we arrived at her destination, which was in completely the opposite direction to where I first intended to go, that the fun started. Marion couldn't get out. The stiff and misaligned passenger door resisted all attempts to open it. Going round to her side of the car I prised the door open but couldn't decide whether to help Marion out or turn away as she struggled to preserve her modesty. As she swivelled off the seat a pair of magnificent legs with all the trimmings came into full view and it was then I realised that there were things, other than engines, that needed to be studied and learned about. However, my learning curve in this field became much longer and drawn out than I would have liked as word got around about the state of my Standard Flying 8A. In any case, other people turned up in newer cars and for some unknown reason the most attractive girls preferred to risk death by roaring off on the back of motor bikes. Even the leftovers preferred to wait for the bus.

It was while enjoying one of my rare social outings at the Brancepeth Youth Club that the first opportunity occurred for me to execute a complete breakdown on my own. A local man arrived at the village hall bemoaning that his Austin van had stopped on a nearby road but he had managed to get a lift from a passing motorist to the Youth Club. That evening I was with a local girl named Susan. Although it had taken me several weeks to engage her in some meaningful conversation I had no hesitation in telling her that something really major had cropped up.

Despite being improperly dressed for the occasion I promptly set off with the stranded motorist in tow to my Standard Flying 8A which was parked adjacent to the steps of the village hall. For self-preservation purposes I never went anywhere without a good range of tools and a tow rope: the tow rope being available if I had needed someone to help me. We set off in earnest but I could see by the face of the stricken motorist that he viewed the chance of us getting back to his vehicle as being rather slim. Despite his misgivings, after two or three miles, we came across his Austin van. By coincidence it was the same model as the one I had used for my driving test. It didn't take long for me to get under the bonnet and diagnose a loose wire to the distributor condenser, which I repaired. He may have been surprised when the vehicle burst into life but it was only what I expected, although I was slightly relieved. The motorist announced that he was a friend of Alan Bromley's and he would arrange for me to have a drink. How he managed to avoid me for the next 30-odd years is of some considerable amazement. Nevertheless, it was the experience that I had enjoyed.

As I returned to the village Youth Club an unusual atmosphere had developed and people were saying that President Kennedy had been shot but were unsure about what might or might not be happening. I still remember that night but for a completely different reason. My abiding memory is how I bared back the orange wire on the condenser and trapped it under the remains of the terminal, tightening the nut with a pair of pliers, refitting the distributor cap and how that green Austin A35 van started and drove away. My first breakdown had been completed and the phone had not even rung once.

The following day I was quick to extol the virtue of my skills as a breakdown mechanic but Alan didn't seem impressed and I was left repairing cars and thinking that I would never be involved in breakdown work. I did get the occasional chance to go to people's houses and face cars that were reluctant to start. Sometimes these were old and decrepit and it was generally assumed that I would fail to get them going but I was full of self-confidence and very little deterred me. In all, I worked for nearly five years at Bromley's Garage and served probably the most thorough and broad-based apprenticeship that anyone could ever experience. I not only learned about cars, I also learned about many aspects of life and the numerous things that make up the running of a business.

One day 20 tons of spare cement arrived and Alan decided we should re-lay the stable floor. What a difference it made, having a flat floor, we were now four inches nearer the already low roof. It made an unbelievable difference, even though in our haste to put the concrete down we didn't move as many items as we should have done. The workbench, for example, was four inches lower and the drill stand entombed by the feet forever. Not only did we finish up with a flat floor but also one Monday morning I arrived for work to find two girders sticking out into mid-air from the side of the garage yard, supported by two brick pillars. We had a fully air-conditioned under-body inspection area. In true Bromley's Garage fashion working conditions were wonderful, providing the weather was warm and it didn't rain. It was the first time that we had been able to stand under a vehicle while carrying out repairs.

Whilst most of my time was taken up with work involving cars and any other mechanical vehicle that needed my valuable assistance, I had always been interested in the game of cricket. I would like to have played cricket at school but was never there on the days when the matches were played. However, Brancepeth village had one of the finest village teams in the area that played the game to a high standard and observed the spirit of the rules in every way. I longed to be able to play in this team; I would turn up and practice with the village professionals and would chase all over the field gathering the ball up for just two or three minutes of batting. I even helped to cut the grass. Then one Saturday my chance came. One of the players had fallen from his motorcycle and the chap who ran the team, the village plumber by the name of John Garbett, told me to go and get my gear. He was surprised to find that I had been carrying it in my vehicle all season.

Like my first breakdown, I can recall my first cricket match, how I batted last and was left three not out, but I was in the team and it was some years before I eventually worked my way through to opening the batting. Even though I was a mediocre player I always employed the same dogged determination that I employ in life generally. I hated to be out, I could bat over after over and not lose my wicket, provided I did not make the rash move of trying to score runs. This sometimes suited the team if we were struggling. If we were not struggling, my so-called team mates at the other end would get rid of me somehow. I continued to play until the team lost its village ground some 20 years later. During my playing years I always feel grateful that some of the better players tolerated me so well. I still savour the atmosphere of a village cricket match in the middle of summer, the smell of recently cut grass and the sound of the ball striking the bat, all in the cool of the evening.

After the learning experiences of my grandfather's Standard 8A, which not unexpectedly found its final resting place in a Willington scrap yard, my move to a Ford 100E van, purchased from a local pig farmer, opened up an endless range of possibilities. Nevertheless, the demise of the Standard Flying 8A was sad in many ways. The sadness in its passing has grown greater over the years as the memories of my grandfather's treasured pride and joy is forever etched in my memory. I have to be realistic and say that when I took ownership of it the car was already on its last legs. It was 16 years old, chronically unreliable, rained in everywhere, which in turn had rotted the wooden floor boards; its oil consumption was at least a pint every 15 miles, which was replenished using second hand oil from the daily garage services. The brakes, which were always a challenge being cable and rod operated, were now down to working on the front nearside wheel only; but all these things were easily forgotten. There was not a final straw or final nail in the coffin, I would have had to persevere with it if the 100E hadn't come along because the pig farmer had decided to upgrade to a Morris 1000 pick-up, which allowed him to keep his pigs clear of the passenger compartment and also to enjoy the luxury of four forward gears and an overhead valve engine. The whole episode brought dismay from my grandmother who, being non-mechanical, failed to understand how they had used the vehicle successfully for over 14 years and I had appeared to destroy it in less than 14 months. Having got rid of one problem vehicle my new transport still posed another, the impossible task of ridding it of the smell of pigs. After various abortive attempts I decided to exchange one smell for another by painting the entire inside with a thick coat of white gloss paint, which seemed to do a reasonable job. Ownership of the Ford 100E van meant I was able to travel at night and fully expected to get back. I also found that some members of the Youth Club, who hadn't bothered or been able to pass a driving test, pronounced themselves friends. They presumed that I would transport them to and from whichever social function I decided to attend on the one night of the week when we would all go out, which was usually a Saturday. The usual haunt was one of the dance halls in Newcastle upon Tyne, some 30 miles to the north.

I decided the best course of action was to make a small charge for this service, which surprisingly enough they agreed to pay. It didn't take me long to work out how many people I needed to have a totally free night out and a few shillings left over. I even surprised myself at the number of people that could cram into a Ford 5-cwt van. On one occasion I recall getting stopped by the police who made me remove four passengers before I could drive away, but once the police had disappeared I just drove back and put them back in, because I really didn't want to lose the fares. The other proviso of this early business arrangement was that the journey was only guaranteed one way. Should I get fixed up with someone from the dance hall I didn't want seven or eight yobs in my van cramping my style by offering advice of an embarrassing nature. I now know why they weren't too concerned because usually it was them who would get fixed up, not me. So, by the law of averages, they were on to a good value-for-money transport arrangement. Some 40 years later, during the course of a breakdown, I was reunited with one of the passengers who remembered travelling in the back of the van with her sister. She remembered particularly as it was the only way to get out on a Saturday night but on arriving at the Mayfair Ballroom at Newcastle they had to scurry of to the Ladies and re-dowse themselves with strong perfume to get rid of the van smells.

This arrangement seemed to lumber on for a goodly while with no end of different Youth Club members who would take advantage of the transport arrangements. During this time, much to the amusement of my passengers, especially the female ones, I was slowly developing my techniques at luring some of the many hundreds of attractive girls that used to go to the Newcastle Majestic Dance Hall. I had even, at my mother's suggestion, bless her, been measured and fitted at Burton's Tailors with a new suit. It was dark brown in colour with just a delicate speckle, but best of all I'd had it specially manufactured with a loud pink lining. If I left my jacket unbuttoned on the dance floor it would really catch the eye. I used to love going to the Majestic I think most of all because it had a live band and was always chock-a-block and it didn't have alcohol. Nevertheless, 75% of the people would have had six pints to drink before they went in but it used to get absolutely crammed and there were never any fights or even dust-ups, something that would send me running a mile. Being a driver I always gave alcohol a miss so I was often in the premises before all the best girls were taken. My technique was to move in swiftly, get the girl on to the dance floor and tell her what a good motor mechanic I was, or something like that. Then, as she went back to her friends, move to the other side of the dance hall and start again. If things didn't work out well it would often be worth trying a girl who was not 'spot on' as I would make the foolish assumption that she would be more desperate to get up and dance and less reluctant to walk off.

However, this proved a horrible route as inevitably the rougher women are the more snappy and nasty and it can take ages to recover from a verbal outburst from somebody like that. This would send me back to Youth Club friends to recharge my mental batteries. Quite often I would meet someone who was quite nice and made the Saturday night worthwhile, but meeting them again was not easy. First of all Newcastle was a centre where people came to from many miles away and they could easily be 20 or 30 miles the other side of Newcastle and I had paying passengers to take home. So I just hoped they would turn up the following week, which sometimes they did and sometimes they didn't. If they didn't live too far away I would perhaps arrange to go to the pictures the following Sunday night and, looking back, once they had had a Saturday night with me and a Sunday night, that was enough for anybody. But completely undaunted I just resumed operations the following weekend.

After all I was still making a profit or that was at least until one memorable Saturday night while walking round the edge of the dance floor with a friend called Sam, a Youth Club member that I got on well with. He tapped me on the shoulder and said, "Look, there's two over there by themselves." And we quickly manoeuvred the girls into the centre of the dance floor. I had found out that if they were near the sides they could easily slip away, so we had covered that one early on. As the two girls came out of the shade and into the better light, I realised that on this occasion I had got the best one. So many times in the past it was me who finished up with the 'dead duck'. In fact, I could not believe my eyes, she was tall and very pretty and had a most wonderful smile and she told me her name was Barbara. She asked my name which made a change as I had often had to tell them who I was and then shout it a second time to make certain I wasn't called 'Ed' or 'Ted'.

We managed to have a good conversation and she seemed quite interested as to how I had got to the evening and who my friend was, she even remarked on the pink lining of my jacket. After about 10 minutes her friend tapped her on the shoulder which was the usual sign of 'we're off' but instead they huddled together for a few minutes and her friend left and so Sam had no option but to retire from the scene leaving me and Barbara alone, which was fine my me. I was even more amazed after another 10 or 15 minutes when a Jim Reeves song 'I Love You Because' was being played and she moved forward for a smooch. I had had this situation on one or two occasions but not with somebody as attractive and nice and somebody with what appeared to be a little bit of enthusiasm. She didn't half cuddle in. Being a little shell shocked I'd lost the plot, especially when she asked if we could go and sit somewhere and would I buy her a drink, which would be of the orange juice or lemonade variety because that was all that was sold.

We then sat in some of the comfortable seats away from the hustle and bustle. I had had a sort of girlfriend from the Youth Club once but Barbara really unsettled me. I couldn't avoid looking at her eyes and she kept talking, asking about me and talking to me and the time just seemed to fly. We went and had another dance or two because the music was still smoochy then we sat back down in some secluded corner and started kissing and cuddling. When it came to kissing her I was confident of my technique which I had developed earlier when learning to siphon petrol. I then felt this firm hand on my shoulder and a chap in uniform said. "Any more of that and you're out, son." It's hard to imagine but the discipline of the place was such that we had just breached etiquette. Not only was the place dry of alcohol but the code of practice would have done a Catholic church proud but it was still so popular that if you didn't go before 9 o'clock you didn't get in.

I then popped a leading question, could I transfer her home? She said that would be absolutely wonderful but I would have to take her friend as well because she lived two doors off. Nevertheless I tried to look on the bright side and sure enough her friend jumped out and disappeared, leaving me the delicacy of a good night kiss. On this occasion I'd had my wits about me to make a further appointment to see her later in the week, before I had to hustle back to Newcastle to pick up Sam and five other people. They'd all had a terrible night and they gave me a fair old ribbing, which I have to say I thoroughly enjoyed.

After giving my van an inside valet and freshening it up by tipping a few drops of solvent into the seams, I duly turned up for my Thursday night date. I thought the prospects of her being there were good seeing she told me to go to the end of the street only 50 yards from her house that was at Low Fell and true enough she was there in all her glory. After a fairly exciting night (at least from my point of view) I suddenly realised that I would have to forego my paying passengers for I was sure my new found friendship with Barbara May would be a better bet, so the cheap trips to Newcastle for other people had to be put on hold. Over the coming weeks we got to know each other quite well. I could really only afford to see Barbara once during the week and once on a weekend but we used to go to different places and she was always happy to be transferred about in my 100E van. She never once complained about it but it was summer and she didn't have to endure the poor heater as well as an odd smell. But, with hindsight, despite the fact that I thought she was absolutely wonderful she was so attentive and seemingly interested in everything I did, I was far too naïve and hopeless to retain a girl of this quality.

I had no idea how a girl worked. I knew how to start a car from cold; it is just a matter of applying the right amount of choke and being steady on the throttle, trying to put on too many revs early results in the whole thing extinguishing. Whereas a warm engine that is already flooded requires a different technique to get it fired up involving full throttle and plenty of revs. However, as far as Barbara was concerned I didn't know if I was going to be dealing with a cold start or a hot start or no start at all. I suppose I knew where all the controls were positioned but like looking at the dashboard of a sports car I didn't know whether the controls were push or pull or needed turning to the left or right; then again some switches go up and down. Anyhow with my occupation I would have been worried that I might have left oil on her knickers. This was a vain hope. I suppose I impressed Barbara with some of my contacts. Among other things I managed to get two complimentary tickets to go to see the Beatles when they were at their height. However, after five or six months and even after I had repaired the handbrake on her father's Morris Oxford, she blew me out and that was it really. I suppose the feeling was just like someone who has been sitting in a sports car twice a week while they save up to buy it, being of a favourite colour and a favourite type. Then one day they go round to put a deposit down and find that somebody has bought the car and driven it away and their dreams are shattered. I remember it was a Thursday night and I really felt terrible but I thought by the Saturday I would rustle up a van load of people and get back to the Majestic and warm up again on something short of spot on.

But, alas, other people had also gone their own way. One or two had got their own vehicles, many had got their own sleeping partners and I suddenly felt a bit isolated socially, but worst of all my Saturday night taxiing business was now defunct and my suit with its flashy lining was left on a coat hanger.

As I was nearing the end of my apprenticeship I became disillusioned with my working surroundings. We were still working on the same old cars and I still hadn't fulfilled my desire to do more breakdown and accident work. Like all apprentices of my age, I felt that I deserved more pay than I was getting, plus I was still having to go to the shop, still lighting the fire in the winter, though of course I had progressed to picking up spare parts when the garage ran out, using the garage runabout.

I always had a tremendous desire to be involved in motor sport. I bought and read all the magazines and knew as far as driving was concerned I was different because I wasn't frightened of sliding or skidding. In fact I relished driving at high speed on ice and snow covered roads. Whenever it snowed I would regularly go out late at night and cover 50 miles as fast as possible. No matter which vehicle I tackled, I never had any problems with the gears or controls, yet in my present position I would be lucky if I was able to watch a motor sport event never mind taking part. I began to look for a more suitable job. There were always plenty of vacancies, getting a better job would not be difficult as I had experienced considerable responsibility even at my young age, but selecting an appropriate position appeared harder.

Along with the rest of my age group I had long since departed the village youth club, which was closed down by an over-zealous village Rector. We felt that he seriously over-reacted when somebody rode a 500cc BSA motor cycle up the fire escape steps and into the main village hall, leaving tyre marks on the newly laid out badminton court. We agreed that the incident should have warranted a verbal warning, but the Rector, who was head of the Parish Council, thought differently. He always seemed pained that the youth club attendance on a Friday night was five times the size of his Sunday congregation, so an exciting chapter of village life was brought to an end. In any case, I was now an enthusiastic member of Durham Automobile Club (DAC), which was one of the largest motor clubs in the North East and had a number of rally drivers who would regularly take part in the Monte Carlo Rally.

Whilst attending a DAC club evening I overheard a conversation that the nearby Ford dealership, which also ran one of the largest breakdown and recovery services in the county, were looking for an additional breakdown mechanic. I could hardly believe this so the following evening I dashed from Willington to Durham City to sound out the situation. When arriving at this large and very well organised dealership I knew that I would have to think carefully about the job application procedure. Fortunately, after dealing with customers and coming into contact with many people who were both friendly and intelligent, I had started to develop one or two negotiating skills.I worked out that the correct procedure would be to approach a man in a white coat in a hut marked 'Foreman's Office' and ask if the rumour was true that they were requiring a breakdown person.

My enthusiasm was dampened when this man, who looked very senior, told me that it was nothing to do with him, he ran the workshop. I would have to see the boss and he would not be in until ten in the morning. I left with mixed feelings that perhaps there was not a vacancy and I would not ever get a job. It never occurred to me that I could have telephoned and made an appointment to see the head of the company, instead I just managed to be present the next day at 11 o'clock. I simply turned up, boiler suit and all, and asked to see the boss about a job. I can remember being absolutely amazed and so nervous when a pretty and well turned out girl working in reception, said, "He'll see you now, follow me." However, as I approached what was in essence the Managing Director's office, he must have seen what was coming and came straight out to meet me, thereby avoiding the embarrassment of dirty feet and oily overalls in his immaculate office. My second job interview was then carried out in the corner of a large reception area that was also adorned with a brand new Ford Cortina GT. This was the first and last time I would ever be interviewed in a show room.

It seemed a coincidence that the person who interviewed me was called Alan. This time his full name was Alan Able and with a few other names his initials were ANSA, which he'd used to form the company name of Ansa Motors. Sir, as I was always to address him, was tall and of course immaculately dressed. Unlike Alan Bromley, he had employed hundreds of other people over the years and was a skilled interviewer. He was therefore not bothered what I looked like nor how good my formal qualifications were but he was obviously able to work out what I was about and whether or not I was going to be able to do the job. Mr. Able's preciseness impressed me and his stern manner concealed what I was later to find to be quite an astute sense of humour. I had just turned 21 years of age and part of the job would be heavy recovery so I was slightly concerned that my weakness at driving extremely large vehicles would catch me out. However, he wasted no time in coming to a decision and asked me how soon I could start. I gave him the reply of, "A week on Monday," hoping that no one else would come along who could start sooner. Mr. Able shook my greasy hand and I walked out of the showroom. We had not really firmed up on working hours and had only briefly discussed a rate of pay but I was so dumbfounded and delighted at getting the job that I couldn't care less. If I didn't have any money at all I felt my Mum would still provide me with a meal every night.

I then had to work my way back to Willington having officially been out collecting spare parts. It was hard to conceal my excitement but I had to do so until the next morning when, for the first time in my life, I had to hand in my notice. I knew this wouldn't go down well because after all I was the only mechanic that Bromley's Garage had and I was doing at least 60% of the work. Despite the chilly atmosphere, the following Saturday lunch time, after working a week's notice, I loaded my meagre tool kit into my Ford van, picked up my tea mug and drove out of the back yard of Bromley's Garage for the last time.

After a few months I bumped into Alan Bromley and he had returned to his normal friendliness; he'd found a replacement member of staff and as time went by we became true friends. It came as an awful shock when he was killed in a road accident in 1987. Alan was someone I greatly respected, someone I owed so much to and it filled me with sadness that I would never see him again.

# CHAPTER III

The job I was about to embark on as a breakdown and recovery mechanic was about as far removed from my previous surroundings as can possibly be imagined. Not only was I working in a highly respected Ford dealership, I would also be taking responsibility for the breakdown service during my tour of duty. A few nights before I was due to start my first shift I took a discreet look at some of the recovery vehicles. These were parked in a side road near to the main premises. I was amazed at the size of the heavy recovery vehicle and all its equipment and even the medium recovery vehicles were much larger than anything I had worked with. I began to feel apprehensive.

My tour of duty for each shift was from 5 o'clock at night until 8 o'clock the next morning. During this time I would answer the telephone, take details of the job, lock the workshop doors and transfer the telephone to a nearby filling station that was owned by the same company. I would have to select an appropriate vehicle and do the job. I was also responsible for costing any cash jobs that arose during my shift, collect the money and at all times process any relevant paperwork. While a skilled motor mechanic working 40 hours would receive £14 or £15 per week, for my job I was to be paid £34 for each week's work, although of course I would be available for breakdown work for at least 105 hours each week, which was a fantastic wage in any walk of life. I underwent a week's training and my apprehensiveness faded.

As I arrived at 8.30 on my first Monday morning I was fizzing with excitement, thinking only of how I would soon be driving breakdown trucks. What I didn't anticipate was the political minefield that I was entering in a business that employed 15 or 20 people. I soon realised that several people already working with the company had wanted the job I now had and for them this meant the end of weekend working and overtime. It didn't take me long to work out why I had been selected rather than the promotion of existing staff. One or two disappointed members of staff became despondent, acting positively nasty towards me. They remained that way until eventually going off to do something else. I was to be trained by a breakdown mechanic called George who had considerable experience in this sort of work but who was already approaching the end of his use-by date. He had developed other interests including a nurse from the hospital and he was looking forward to me taking on some of his work.

I soon realised that one or two members of staff had been re-named because of either their personality or their mannerisms. The company Service Manager had spent considerable time driving army vehicles during the war and it was almost impossible to have a conversation with him without the war cropping up. I suppose I should not have been surprised therefore when he referred to one of the young apprentices as 'Rommel'. Not knowing what the real Rommel looked like nor how good he might be at repairing vehicles, I couldn't make a comparison with this poor young lad who had been saddled with such a ridiculous nickname.

A fanatical Middlesbrough supporter who had an uncanny resemblance to a character on the popular television series 'The Army Game' ran the stores department. So everyone referred to him as 'Bisley'. While Bisley knew the part number of just about every part on any Ford car, his manner of dealing with people depended not only on their attitude to his beloved football team but also whether they sympathised with his plight of suffering from a bad case of haemorrhoids. I was astonished to see a customer approaching with his wallet in his hand preparing to buy spare parts that were obviously in stock, only to be turned away in fury when he asked Bisley why he was scratching his backside. It could have been worse; he could at the same time have pointed out how badly Middlesbrough had played recently. Either way, this poor chap was sent 20 miles to the next Ford dealer to get his spare parts. Whereas when another customer, who had probably learned his lesson the hard way, turned up carrying a new brand of cream and sincere commiserations on the 7-1 defeat of the previous Saturday, he would not only be supplied with every spare part he needed down to the last washer and split pin but he would also be offered a 10% discount for loyalty.

Another of Bisley's obsessions was his overwhelming desire to win those ridiculous Spot the Ball competitions. On one such occasion he was so adamant that he had seen the picture and knew where the ball was he convinced most of the garage to go for a cross, so 15 or so crosses appeared in a certain place. As it became time for the results to be announced, Bisley had almost already spent the prize money, only for it to be confirmed on that particular picture that the ball had ricocheted and was on top of the grandstand roof some 50 yards, or six inches across the photograph, away from where all the crosses were. He felt he was completely vindicated when in small print he noticed a short statement in the newspaper saying, "Last week there were no winners."

In many ways the garage was equipped with some of the best and most skilled staff I have ever come across. It also had people with a tremendous sense of humour, people who were miserable and grumpy, the odd "jobsworth" and even the occasional person who was light fingered, but for me it was a perfect working environment. How they perceived me was irrelevant. I had always been an independent sort of person; I didn't need the affection or reassurance of work colleagues. I was far more single-minded and determined than the whole lot put together, so I can't say that I immediately developed much in the way of friendship. I was to be working in an extremely responsible position and in many cases it was best to keep a distance from one or two staff. However, I struck up quite a good working relationship with a young stores assistant called John who was Bisley's long-suffering assistant. John was always quick to show me where the necessary parts were, whereas Bisley would just grunt as he scratched his backside.

The layout of the premises was a large fully fitted workshop adjoining a rather grand showroom. To the side of the workshop was the stores area that was always closely guarded by Bisley. To the side of the workshop was an 8 ft. by 12 ft. room with stone walls and wooden slatted benches, with a large stone sink at one end. This was the canteen area for the entire work force. At one end of the wooden benches were a couple of rear car seats. When I asked why these were at one end, I was told, "That's where George sleeps at night." and I realised that it would also be where I would be getting my head down between breakdowns. The night shift was obviously so drawn out that workers were allowed to pass the time with a snooze. I had already begun to think that this arrangement would have to improve.

Another area in need of change was the position of the telephone. It was in the Service Manager's office some 20 yards from the canteen, so when the phone rang during the night George had to first of all hear it, then scramble across the workshop floor to pick up the receiver. I was later to adjust the system so that it rang on the stores counter, which was only a few feet away from the canteen. If I was really tired I found that standing the telephone on an old biscuit tin increased the noise level. When I look back it seems so ridiculous that we didn't just extend the wire and have the telephone in the canteen during the night.

Ten days after moving to the job of a lifetime, I started my first night shift at 5 p.m. on the Wednesday. The plan was that I would work seven nights, followed by 24 hours of rest and relaxation, followed again by six day shifts of 8 o'clock in the morning until 5 o'clock at night including weekends. This work pattern was to continue for the next seven years. The shift opposite me would be covered by an existing breakdown mechanic called Albert, who was some years older than me and who had a rather fiery temper and a strange attitude towards customers. I was rather pleased that I only came across him at the change of shifts. George, in the meantime, had reverted to permanent days as he had now moved in with his nurse. He didn't see the bunk in the canteen as being a viable option to the comfort of her bed.

By ten past five on that first shift I was down in the centre of Durham attending to a Ford Corsair that was having trouble with gear selection. It didn't take me long to realign the gear linkage and get the man on his way. In the excitement I recall leaving my toolbox on the side of the road and having to double back. Fortunately, the toolbox didn't appeal to anyone passing and was still intact on my return. Even though the Ansa Motors breakdown service was not particularly large it was one of the biggest and most respected operations in the North East and at 21 years of age I was in charge of it: at least for the next

15 hours. I realised after being in charge for five hours that I had completed more breakdowns in that time than I'd managed in the previous five years.

The vehicle I would regularly use was one of a pair of diesel long wheelbase Land Rovers (which we always referred to as L/Rs). These vehicles were equipped with a Harvey Frost breakdown crane which, in practice, was a metal tripod with a piece of wire rope attached to a hook at one end and a hand winch at the other. Everyone used to rave about the efficiency of these L/R recovery units but I had already formed an opinion that they were unreliable. This was even before I saw that Bisley kept four spare half shafts tucked away in his stores. It always puzzled me why the consumption of half shafts on these L/Rs was so high. I was the one who pushed the vehicles on a bit yet never once suffered a half shaft failure. It was six or seven years later when I realised that the reason that L/Rs broke half shafts so frequently was because people were clumsy with the transmission handbrake. They would apply the handbrake before the vehicle had come to a standstill, putting a phenomenal reverse load on the shafts. It would then brake some five minutes later when the vehicle was in forward motion. I was probably saved embarrassment because I didn't bother much with the handbrake, often stopping the engine and just leaving the vehicle in gear. When I tried to explain to these drivers what was happening, I was faced with a whole lot of abuse.

The less said about the crane the better because if the car wasn't damaged when you went to move it, it certainly would be afterwards. That's why we moved 95% of cars by towing them with a length of rope. It was some 10 years before I realised how ridiculous those L/Rs were for breakdown work. We should have used vehicles which were cheaper to buy and cheaper to run. These would have done the job a whole lot better. However, in fairness, each of these Land Rovers would cover around 50,000 miles each year. It was not unusual to do 200 miles during a shift. At that time there were no mobile phones and we didn't have two-way radios, so it was quite common to travel 20 miles to jump start a car, return to the workshop, then go back 20 miles to start another car in the next street.

Our work came from many sources. The AA patrols were very poor. Patrolmen, many recruited from the armed forces, were dressed in a strange shade of khaki. They worked during daylight hours, which in the winter was 9a.m. to 3p.m. and only slightly longer in the summer. Predominantly, they were still using motorcycle patrolmen to formally salute an approaching vehicle bearing an AA badge. So, unless it was little more than a light bulb change, contracted garages like ourselves were called out to do the job. However, changes were ahead and one or two mini vans would soon be seen patrolling the roads. These vans were painted in what was to become their distinctive yellow livery. Changes were indeed afoot. One or two AA patrols were even experimenting with the wearing of boiler suits to see if such a garment would be suitable for working on cars. They should have asked us, particularly as the rest of the motor trade had been wearing such clothing for 75 years! There was one useful bonus when a patrol changed from a motorcycle to a van. The patrolman would dispense with his heavy overcoat, an object not unlike the garment worn by Mussolini when he visited Siberia. It weighed about a stone but was extremely warm and cosy; the one I acquired lasted for years.

Because of its design I guessed that the early AA uniform was derived from First World War Army issue. What I and other breakdown staff used to wear could only have originated from the National Coal Board. Whilst today everyone is neurotic about working in high visibility reflective garments that can be seen miles away, we were always equipped in dark blue boiler suits usually covered in oil and grease. To protect us from adverse weather conditions we were issued with black donkey jackets with no reflection whatsoever. A black woolly hat was considered vital to protect sensitive ears against biting winds. We must have been invisible in the dark. This warm clothing was worn week in and week out until it eventually became shiny with the oil and grease. I don't remember a donkey jacket ever being washed; it was just worn until it rotted away. Donkey jackets were fully functional; they kept out the rain and cold and had nice big pockets that carried lots of tools.

The RAC, also motorcycle-mounted, had barely a presence and most work was passed to garages. One or two motorists, who fell foul of mechanical failure or anything else, would attempt to make a private arrangement. However, the cost of calling out a breakdown service was always considered to be on the high side. So this part of the business was relatively small. I quickly learned it was better not to bother doing the job if there was a risk of not being paid. Sometimes people would say they had money to pay, only for me to find them 'skint' on arrival. I soon learned how to drive away without any consideration for who they were or the mess they were in. Much heavy breakdown and recovery work came about from a wheels-within-wheels association. Though it didn't represent a large percentage in numbers, each heavy breakdown job seemed to take forever, sometimes all day or all night, whereas the car jobs would come and go.

I hadn't been doing the job many days when I began to come into contact with the police who were valued providers of work. Most of the lucrative work, both for cars and heavy vehicles, came from police involvement. I soon discovered why Bromley's Garage got little or no police accident work. Alan wasn't up to speed with a system that required us to 'look after' any police officer who provided us with a lucrative repair job. His vehicle would be treated to a service now and again and the invoice lost in the system.

I should have realised how the system worked because for all the years on the farm my parents had always supplied the local PC with the occasional half a dozen fresh eggs and a chicken at Christmas. This ensured we never had any problems and poachers wouldn't dare come within 10 miles of the farm. I understand it was common practice for the local police officer to get a bit of fresh meat from the butcher and a loaf of bread from the bakers now and again. Fighting crime is thirsty work so a pint of beer would be left on the wall at the back of the local pub just after the 10 o'clock closing time. These were standard perks of the job, since at that time the police were poorly paid. It is worth reminding us that these were fine upright police officers who wouldn't tolerate any breach of the law. They very easily put the fear of God into anybody who tried to break that law. No youngster would dare set a lip up to them. In those days the law was about stopping crime and arresting criminals and various perks of the job only strengthened the police officer's will to see that his neighbourhood was well policed.

As the stakes increased and other garages tried to muscle in, rather unsuccessfully, it was not unusual for a police officer to find 100 cigarettes left on his seat. I doubt if it made any great difference because I suspect that a few other garages were also on the same system so it just meant that the only beneficiary was the police officer who got to all the good jobs. It was said to me, often in jest, that a successful police officer in the 1950s and 1960s should have been submitting a separate tax return. At one point it got so silly that after the cars had been cleared from a road accident, you couldn't get in the garage entrance for police officers looking for cigarettes. Often ill feeling would break out when one officer would get someone else's entitlement.

This all came to an abrupt end when a Chief Superintendent came to see our intrepid leader, pointing out that this sort of thing had to stop. Some one-minute-and-30-seconds later I was called to the Managing Director's office and that was it, the system had gone. Inwardly this pleased me because it had all become ridiculous, what did not go to the police was going to other people who should not have had anything. The system was abused by anyone who could grab a packet of cigarettes. Heavy smoking had become a habit within the company. When word got around that the system no longer operated work appeared to thin out for a couple of weeks, then normality returned.

After three or four months I had really started to feel at home in the job and while every minute was a steep learning curve I had started to develop some fascinating insight into life evolving on a 24-hour basis seven days a week. Just down the road from the main workshop was the company's 24-hour filling station that had state-of-the-art vending machines dispensing hot drinks at all hours. It was amazing the type of people these premises attracted. Sons of wealthy Durham businessmen would congregate in their new Mini Coopers, Viva GTs and other too powerful cars. These people became firm friends of mine, even though at the time they were absolute young tearaways. I suppose they respected my skills and the job I did which was a life so different from theirs and yet so interesting to me. They proved to be good customers as they frequently crashed and overturned their cars. These lads always seemed to be adorned with pretty girls who were just as headstrong and reckless. Every weekend the conversation would revolve around which hospital someone was in or who was the latest to have been killed.

This was a time when people knew how to live life, although at times it seemed that life was very cheap. Not only did cars not have seat belts but there wasn't any part of the dashboard that wouldn't put a hole in the unfortunate person who fell against it. Driving whilst under the influence of alcohol was commonplace. The skill was not getting caught. These reckless, feckless people were part of a scene that I couldn't be part of, so I just looked on.

## CHAPTER IV

The North East in the 1960s was well up the league of hard gangsters who thrived around the industry of one-armed bandits. These were the original fruit machines that swallowed sixpences. If the punter was lucky and lined up three cherries in a row, 500 or more coins would fall all over the floor. This was called dropping a jackpot and was the Holy Grail of the play. These machines only paid back a small percentage of what was put into them. They were placed in pubs and clubs and it wasn't unusual for them to be fed sixpences for every minute the establishments were open. The agreement to have a machine in a pub or club was that if the licensee didn't allow the machine it would be best for him not to walk down a dark alley. Gangs would fight over the best sites and even over the best position of a bandit in a given club.

So, in essence, these machines were simply cash collection points for gangsters who drove around in big Jaguars with a boot full of sixpences. Often the vehicles were so weighed down that the rear suspension would be in a state of collapse. One such gangster was Angus Sibbert who was found lying beside a car full of sixpences; he had a bullet hole in his head. I'm not certain whether he was one of the many gangsters who suffered car problems but I certainly came into contact with what could be described as the wrong sort of people. But I thought they were wonderful because they always paid promptly with a big handful of sixpences. Usually, when the bill was paid, there was always plenty of money left over. I often compared this to daytime jobs where I've seen a mother empty a child's piggy bank to get the £1 to pay for a jump-start.

Unlike many motorists these hard men were always stone sober no matter what time of day they were at the wheel. Because the only drink/drive test was a driver's ability to walk straight, driving with a belly full of beer was the norm most nights. Having an accident is always a bit unfortunate, but if a driver were injured and taken to hospital that was fortunate because he would not be asked to carry out the mandatory test of walking along a straight line.

It has often been said about the 1960s that it was a time of great freedom and the final release of tension following the Second World War. In reality it was the time when many people's personality and character came to the fore. People who contained great character always surrounded me. These were often those who in today's academic system would not be rated, but they were individuals who in their own way were extremely clever, very innovative and true survivors who depended on nothing but their own sharpness and wit. One such character, who was part of the fixtures and fittings of Durham night life even though in some ways he was attached to a bracket on the edge of life, was Colin P. Jones. He described himself as the only true Durham taxi driver and in just a few ways he was probably right.

He owned a London-type black cab and his company was aptly named 'Durham Taxis' even though he had just the one vehicle. There was no automatic entitlement to a 'Get You Home' service from the AA or the RAC (this was all pre-relay vehicle days). Colin P. would always hover in the vicinity of the garage and filling station and when a stricken car was towed in he would offer his services to get the customers home. His activities were not confined to the vicinity of the workshop and filling station; if he saw a vehicle being towed towards base he would take up the pursuit on the off-chance of securing a job which could be anywhere from a few hundred yards to extreme cases of a few hundred miles. Since this happened on a regular basis it was a valuable 'Add-On' to his existing business. Colin P., like many business people, worked seven days a week, or in his case seven nights. He would usually emerge bleary eyed having just got up at around 9 or 10 o'clock each evening. He was often settled in the filling station and by some weird arrangement would receive his calls on the filling station telephone.

There were many other taxi drivers who would try to work their way into the system with us by virtue of a few shillings handed over for every job, which was something that Colin P. would never do. He was always straightforward and uncomplicated which was a bit of a bind considering he was also a good friend of Sir, and if he thought we had taken a back-hander he would be in the office the next morning complaining. The only result was that we were reminded not to upset him, which was pretty difficult because more often than not he succeeded in upsetting himself. Though he had a fairly good client base, it was of some amusement how nobody would use his taxi more than once. He never liked to think that anyone had scored points at his expense. On one occasion he mistook a 'working girl' for a thoroughly upright citizen and took her on a journey to Sunderland some 15 miles away. As he approached Sunderland his passenger indicated that the method of payment would be through her normal line of work and she suggested he should go round and get into the rear. So shocked by this proposition and realising no money was forthcoming, he simply used the outstanding turning circle of a London taxi and did an immediate

'U' turn almost knocking down two unsuspecting pedestrians. Whereupon he scarpered back to Durham to the very square foot of earth where he'd first picked her up, being of the frame of mind that if he wasn't going to get any money, she certainly wasn't going to get a free trip. Following this encounter Colin P. had to use the facility of our workshop. Leaving the vehicle the girl slammed the door with such vigour that the window dropped down inside its frame. This is a story that was worth telling once, but the problem was that we had to endure endless repeats for the next three years.

In the 1920s motorists had a 1 in 300 chance of being killed or seriously injured on the roads. This had improved slightly by the 1960s but the amount of death and destruction was still devastating. On some Saturday evenings my time would be taken up between 8 p.m. and 2 a.m. doing nothing but towing in badly damaged cars. What happened to the people in the cars was of no concern to me, it was just simply an exciting time and I had a tremendously exciting job.

It was during a call out to an early evening road accident that I came into contact with someone who was to become a life-long friend. Our garage was based opposite the Neville's Cross cross roads, which was the junction of the A690 and the A1 London to Edinburgh road. The junction was controlled by a set of traffic lights with rather inconsistent phasing. On an almost twice-daily basis we were alerted by the familiar crash of metal and the tinkling of broken glass and chrome parts falling to the ground, as yet another pair of cars collided.

As I was busy collecting one of these vehicles, a young straight-out-of-school reporter whom I recognised as being from the Durham Advertiser through a Motor Club encounter arrived on the scene. Astride a very old pedal cycle with no mudguards and no lights he pedalled up to the site of the overturned car, leaned across his handlebars and took out his notebook. Then he made the mistake of asking the attending Police Inspector what had happened. The next thing I saw was this young reporter attempting to recover his cycle from a nearby hedge. His notebook had landed a further eight feet away in some bushes. The officer had taken a dislike to his abrasive attitude and had placed the reporter and his equipment straight into the nearby scenery. Colin gathered up his notebook, surveyed the scene and continued to make notes. This was despite a trickle of blood running down the side of his head where he had made contact with a thorn bush as he struggled to avoid the same fate as his bike.

After the vehicle had been removed and put in the nearby compound, I returned to my 8 by 12 canteen to prepare my sleeping area for an early night. By now it was twenty past nine and I was unsure how much work would appear in the early hours. Since taking over from George I had improved the bunk considerably, replacing the old Ford Consul rear seats with some seat squabs from a Mini. The big advantage of the Mini seats was that they were made completely of sponge and did not contain any sharp springs or brackets. I had trimmed and adjusted them and it became easy for me to drop off to sleep after only a few minutes and not wake up with circles on my back. Suddenly I was startled by the young reporter who was standing just behind me still holding his notebook and determined to complete his assignment. He was obviously not from the North East because he spoke 'properly'. He was more like the people with the fast cars from the filling station, except that he had a notebook and an old pushbike with a buckled wheel. He asked me about the accident and I thought for a second that I might appear as an important breakdown man on the front page of the Durham Advertiser. I later discovered that this young reporter, called Colin Wilson, was on his first week as a junior reporter and had been assigned only to cover Council and Women's Institute meetings and was hoping that the report of a live road accident might get him a few 'Brownie points' back in the office. I don't think the story ever appeared because the Council meeting had taken precedence since the business had involved planning permission for the relocation of a pigeon cree with south-facing nest boxes. Obviously there was going to be a lot of local interest and high circulation figures were expected on this story alone.

Although Colin had been unceremoniously evicted from the scene of this accident, he worked out that he would not be sent packing as quickly if he were riding in my vehicle; this is just what he did almost every night for the next three or four years. He accompanied me through rain, snowstorms and heat waves, arriving around 7.30 each evening after the Council meeting and usually departing around 11 o'clock to his one-room bedsit that he rented from some property racketeer for about three-quarters of his weekly wage. His manner was arrogant to say the least and he was a bit loud, but he was so precise and always knew what he was about and he was always right. Even though he used to get on everyone else's nerves I found him fascinating and he taught me so much, but I always had to make sure that he never engaged Colin P. in any form of conversation otherwise sparks would fly. Colin made a wonderful cup of tea and was often armed with fish and chips for both of us but, more importantly, he learned how to steer a vehicle that was being towed. The common method of recovering a broken down vehicle in those days was by attaching a tow rope and then heading off, sometimes for 20 or 30 miles. I therefore had with me an assistant that Albert my breakdown counterpart did not, in the sense that I could always replace the doddery old motorist with Wislon, as Colin became known, and disappear down a road with a car on tow at unabated speed.

Like me, Wislon was a true motor sport enthusiast so that when we were towing a car across ice or snow-covered roads, the rate of progress had to be seen to be believed. It certainly didn't go down well if there were any passengers in the car that was being towed. In all the years and of the many thousands of cars that we towed together, not once did we put a scratch on either vehicle, unlike the normal motorist who would continually run into the back tow-ball of the Land Rover, often breaking a headlight or two in the process. When this happened I always made a point of getting out and explaining to the motorist that he had just collided with my vehicle and that he had also damaged his own. My manner suggested that he had not noticed the collision, thereby firmly placing the blame and responsibility on him.

I suppose that driving those Land Rovers day and night, winter and summer, over all sorts and conditions of roads, combined with my farm machinery days, sowed the seed that later gave me two British 1600cc Rally Championships and over 40 outright Rally Wins. Although I was a laid back, lazy, day-to-day driver, when the snow came or if it was really wet, I just drove everywhere as fast as possible. Wislon loved it, but nobody else would get in the vehicle with me; they would make any excuse, even walk miles or wait to get a lift from someone else. My driving style was based on safety at speed that involved only using two-wheel drive and always turning the steering wheel well before the corner, thereby allowing the vehicle to lose its speed by going sideways. Once again, in seven years I never left the road or put a mark on an L/R.

There was a chap, George Nichols (known as GN) who lived opposite the workshop. He could often be seen filling his pipe whilst stood on the showroom steps of an evening. One snowy winter morning, at 5 a.m., he hitched a lift to work then gave me a whole load of abuse as we passed the Colpitts Hotel in a controlled slide. He then jumped out at the next junction to await some public transport. Of course there was no reason to believe that public transport would be any safer than travelling with me. I would make the point that he was in greater danger. The bus driver probably stumbled his way to work, cranked his bus up and drove around at two miles an hour terrified he would skid, which inevitably leads to just that situation happening. Whereas I had spent many hours, often with Wislon present, perfecting the art.

One particular night Wislon came stumbling into the workshop covered in snow pronouncing that all radio stations were advising motorists not to venture out. He therefore assumed, quite rightly, that there would be very little work and the roads would be clear for us to go out and practice. We had to keep returning every 20 minutes to see if there were any calls. One of the exercises we embarked on, which was always a constant debate with other breakdown staff, was whether an L/R would travel faster and safer on snow and ice in four-wheel drive or whether it was better to be driving the rear wheels only. We therefore selected an isolated piece of road, about three miles long, which was covered with four or five inches of snow lying on top of ice.

We made several runs using four-wheel drive and several using just rear wheel drive and on all occasions the vehicle was safer and easier to drive and covered the piece of road faster when in two-wheel drive only. However, if there had been steep hills the four-wheel drive would obviously have been of some advantage but because the diesel engine had so little power to spare there was less drag through the transmission and the steering and control of the vehicle was much more precise. It was much easier to steer and I pronounced it much safer to drive. So after this exercise, four-wheel drive was abandoned except for towing duties.

If I was lucky enough to be working a day shift I would think nothing of doing 150 miles or so every night when the roads were appropriate. As the snow started to thaw I was like an animal searching for food and I had to go further into the hills and dales each night to find roads that still contained snow and ice after it had long vanished in the built up areas.

By this time I had purchased a Ford Anglia 105E and had fitted a Cortina GT engine which was a common conversion of the day. It made an excellent vehicle for travelling about the roads and for practising my driving technique as well as being a suitable vehicle for every day transport. In complete contrast to earlier years, the job had provided me with sufficient money to get well into all branches of Motor Sport. However, time was always a problem and would continue to be so. Except while working, each night I had plenty of time between jobs to ensure the Anglia was completely up to scratch in all areas. I could try all sorts of different conversions, drive round the roads the next day and then put them right again the following night.

Like other competitors I was constantly searching for something to make my car go faster. People generally would try almost anything to get extra speed and more success. I came across one rally driver who had a problem with his concentration and claimed that by rigging up some sort of tape player and an ear piece (today we would call it a Walkman) he would then play music in a tempo that was necessary for his driving style. He always claimed that by playing Red River Rock he could go one second a mile faster over a particular downhill section. He would then settle for Matt Munro for some of the road sections through the quieter villages in order not to be booked for excessive speeding. If he was hoping to get me to try the same system he didn't succeed. I just stuck to commonsense things like putting heavy gear oil in my rear shock absorbers.

It was not just in the driving seat that I was strengthening my Motor Sport career. I'd been a member of Durham Motor Club for five or six years and had already served on the Committee. It therefore naturally followed on that I would stand for Chairman and was subsequently voted in, which was at a time when the Club was strong and I was blessed with a nucleus of Committee members who all knew what they were doing. We were able to persuade and appoint Colin Wilson (Wislon) as Club Magazine Editor. Each month he produced a 20-page magazine with about as much effort as it took me to change the oil and filter on a Ford Zodiac. The Club grew in stature and in one particular year was responsible for seven crews entering the Lombard RAC Rally. This confirmed that not only did we have 300 members but there was also strength in depth of competitive drivers.

# CHAPTER V

With spending so much time at work, time management became very important and if there is one thing that has always irritated me it is having to wait in a queue. Quite frankly, my brain is not designed for queuing. I was therefore rather fortunate to find when I needed a haircut I could call on the services of a trainee hairdresser who worked in a salon adjoining the garage. She would pop in after hours, sit me down and treat me to a short back and sides and charge me less than five shillings. We always called her Miss Rankin and everybody in the company would have liked to have taken her to bed. In fact, I am sure she just walked backwards and forwards across the front of the premises in her short skirt to wind us up, but she really was very stunning. As the years have gone by she is the only person who has ever cut my hair. I have enjoyed a haircut at just about every location, not just in a workshop but in a breakdown truck, probably in a lay-by. We have been friends for over 40 years, I suppose it helped that she married someone who worked on farm tractors, but I only ever called her Miss Rankin. Sadly the price has gone from five shillings to ten pounds, but it is more than worth it.

Unlike during my apprenticeship days, I had started to get into contact with more girls in the working environment such as Margaret and Barbara who worked in Reception. In those days it was uncommon for women to be sole car owners and they were very rarely the victims of a breakdown. The best bit being that women had not yet developed the art of dignified elegance when getting in and out of cars, especially the old models with forward opening doors (the cars, that is). What was more common was finding myself in the middle of a domestic situation because the car had broken down and the wife would declare it was completely the husband's fault. Occasionally, some women even had the cheek to say it was their boyfriend's fault. These were obviously women destined to make unsuitable wives.

Albert, my opposite number, was particularly intolerant of these situations. On one Friday evening I arrived to take over and found a customer raising his voice and displaying a ridiculous attitude because his vehicle had been un-repairable at the roadside. His main gripe was that he was under pressure domestically and was complaining in a loud and irate manner that his wife was due to go out to a dinner that she was so looking forward to. He finished his vocal outburst by asking Albert, "What would you do in my position?" to which Albert replied, in no uncertain manner, "No problem at all. I'd go home and make some egg and chips, like I'll be doing in five minutes' time." The event then took a further turn, when his wife asked if there was anywhere she could wash her hands.

There were two small cubicles at the side of the workshop; one had a toilet bowl and the other a small area with a hand basin and towel. Rather than being precise, she had attempted to be diplomatic but in doing so finished up in a cubicle with only a hand basin. Her movements had gone unnoticed until there was an enormous clatter followed by a screech and a further outburst of complaining as she emerged from the washing facilities with a scratch on her head and both knees slightly grazed. She started complaining that the basin had fallen down off its bracket, landing on her knees, but when Albert noticed that her dress was tucked into her smalls at the back, we realised that she had gone into the wrong room. The brackets holding the basin had not been able to take her weight despite the fact that she was only slightly built, which in some ways was a good job. If she had been a heavyweight model we would probably have needed a greased wedge to slide her out of the small room.

This certainly changed the subject of the evening meal and the couple set off down the road on foot, having declined the services of Colin P. who was on stand-by for his first fare of the evening. Leaving the couple's car for repair at a later date, Albert went off to make his own egg and chips.

Most of the female entertainment came by way of a Monday night dance at the Workingmen's Club some yards across the road from the main garage. There were always people congregating before and after the evening and they would even wander into the garage thinking that we were a taxi service. One particular night Bisley was making some sort of visit to his Parts Department looking for a light fitting for his house or probably his spare haemorrhoid cream. From somewhere deep in the back of his domain, three buxom oversized wenches appeared wearing mini skirts that were 14 sizes too small. One of them asked if anyone was going near Ferryhill, which is eight miles south of Durham. Wislon, never slow to miss a trick, assured them that the immaculate black Triumph Mayflower, owned by our intrepid storekeeper and parked just inside the garage entrance, was going in just that direction in a few minutes.

They were informed that the driver was a shy chap and would not want to give them a lift, so they should insist. As Bisley came out of the stores and saw what was happening he went ballistic. Despite his anger, he had no option but to deliver these sex pots eight miles in the opposite direction to where he lived. They had refused to get out of the vehicle and were far too big and drunk for him to handle because he was not the holder of any form of heavy goods licence.

Sometimes we would try to take advantage when there was a dispute. I was alerted at 10.30 p.m. one night by a grinding noise near the traffic lights followed by a yelling and screaming and the slamming of car doors. On walking across I found an MG Magnet displaying 'L' plates and a young chap in the driving seat attempting to get the remains of his gear box working after his rather attractive female pupil had taken the teeth from his first and second gear. We pushed the car into the workshop but there was little that could be done. It became clear that this was not the man's regular sleeping partner but someone with whom he fancied his chances and saw the route to preliminaries by providing a driving lesson. Apart from now being left with a woman who would not go to bed, he was also out of pocket to the tune of a gearbox. He was such an absolutely obnoxious type of character that I finished up pushing the vehicle down the road and told him that once he got third and fourth gear he would be all right provided that he didn't stop. Then I locked the garage doors and went to the nearby filling station to see my 'yuppie' friends.

Some 15 minutes later his distraught student driver reappeared. She had gone to get a bus but it was all too late and she had no money for Colin P.'s taxi. She did not have to do much to persuade me to take her home to Spennymoor and as we came across the first up-gradient, we spotted the stricken MG Magnet stranded by the roadside. I just made sure that we didn't reduce speed but she had the audacity to wave.

Not all women were as well mannered or as grateful for a lift. Another friend and associate, who we always referred to as 'Hovis' mainly because the family engineering company was called 'Brown's', had broken down in his father's Humber. After towing the vehicle to the workshop for repair I was in the process of taking Hovis home in the breakdown Land Rover to the far side of Durham. He had already collected fish and chips for his family. As we started to get out into open country an extremely attractive middle-aged woman who was frantically trying to thumb a lift confronted us. In those days it was always safe to take a lift and people often actively pursued free transport and equally people were willing to stop and help. So this was no big deal. Hovis invited her into the vehicle and she climbed into the middle seat, which instead of having a cushion was the valve box for the Pye Cambridge short wave radio system that we had on trial.

After about a mile or so the radio started to crackle and we remarked how we hoped that the trial would be unsuccessful and maybe we would get a different set with better reception. After several miles she indicated her destination and we stopped and let her out. As she climbed out across the passenger seat we noticed that everywhere was wet. We discovered that she had relieved herself while still on the move. Not only had she damaged the radio valve box but she had also blanched Hovis's fish and chips in the process. He was faced with no other option but to put them in a roadside litter bin. They were last seen going down the footpath in the mouth of a stray Alsatian. I left Hovis searching for somewhere that was open to get his family a new supper and the next day we had to get an engineer to repair the radio valve box.

Sometimes the sight of a pair of legs thumbing a lift can have an unexpected twist. One particular foggy night I stopped to help a damsel in distress only to find it was a rather friendly Scotsman in a kilt. On another occasion I was returning to Durham from Scotch

Corner one summer evening when it was still very light. As I was about to turn on to the A1 an extremely young and elegant girl approached me and asked if I was going to Durham. When I indicated that this was exactly where I was going she said, "Just a minute." and a further seven or eight similar girls ran from behind a hedge and scrambled over the back of the truck. They wouldn't get off so the only thing I could do was to ask them to sit quietly as I drove the 28 miles to Durham on a vehicle that was run on trade plates and was only supposed to be used for vehicle recovery. Fortunately, no one suffered any worse fate than getting covered with oil and grease but for some of the journey I actually thought that if I got caught I might lose my job.

The long-held theory that wrapping round and knotting a genuine nylon stocking can create a replacement fan belt was sometimes worth a try. While it was always worth the experience of seeing the stocking removed, I had little success in making even a temporary repair. However, if this replacement denier fan belt could be made to drive only the water pump then the vehicle can be driven at a steady pace. The problem occurred if the stocking was given too much work to do by being expected to drive both the water pump and the dynamo. We were always full of thoughts and ideas to keep cars on the road. Another common held theory, which had about as much success, was that putting the white of two eggs in with the water could temporarily repair a leaking radiator. The egg white could mix with the water and when it came out through the hole in the radiator it would set like a scrambled egg. These things are always worth a try if you are the motorist but they are not much use if someone is paying for a professional service.

We had not yet entered the era of the suppressed wife driving the domineering husband's car. Just about all women driving cars were independent, self-reliant characters who were usually excellent to deal with, knew what they were about and were nobody's fool. So when they had to call a breakdown service it was us who had to be on our toes to avoid either being embarrassed or feeling inadequate. Whatever their dilemma, women drivers were often in much better humour when the situation did not involve a broken down car. The first time I attended one such lady who was a member of the AA and had arranged for a friend to call for assistance. Her expensive skirt had become jammed when the wind had slammed the driver's door on her Ford Corsair, trapping her in the zero torque locking mechanism. As I arrived I noticed at least 18 inches of the garment was stuck in the door mechanism they were deciding whether she should travel home by running alongside the car. At first I tried to free off the door but the presence of her broad hips stopped me getting anywhere near the latch. She then decided that the only way was to work herself out of her skirt; which she promptly did. Once free of the trapped garment she sat in the passenger seat until I was able to release the door, whereupon she simply re-clothed, thanked me for not damaging the article any more than it was, and the whole party went off full of good humour.

On another occasion I was sitting outside the workshop at our famous cross roads when there was a tremendous blowing of horns and shouting. I saw a car stopped in the middle of the junction. The smart lady at the wheel was becoming increasingly flustered because for some reason she was unable to move. When I ran across to establish why she couldn't move she said, "The clutch has gone loose." It had lost all its fluid and the car was stuck in gear. Because of the gradient she couldn't release the gear lever and the car wouldn't start on the ignition. I told her if she would let me in the driver's side I would solve the problem and get the car clear of the junction. Instead of getting out she opted to scramble over to the passenger side, legs and all. Somehow in her haste and confusion she managed to get one of her suspenders caught on the gear lever. After one attempt at freeing herself she quickly unhooked the offending garment and burst into hysterics, having provided me with such a good floorshow.

Whenever cars overturned on this same junction, which they never seemed to do with any great violence, just a gentle roll, we would often be presented with some wonderful sights as people scrambled out with their dignity far from intact.

As far as my own social contact with the opposite sex was concerned this had somewhat died a death after the Barbara May episode. I soon realised that a girlfriend was all right occasionally but often took up valuable time and could easily become high maintenance with ever increasing running costs. In any case my life had moved on from Bromley's Garage. I was now in a job which in itself took up all the social hours and as far as I was concerned Friday nights and Saturday nights were brilliant nights for working with lots of road accidents and not nights to be wasted in a pub. Even the Majestic Dance Hall had been brushed from my memory.

My social activities tended to be limited to the once-fortnightly visit to the Durham Motor Club which had a fair sprinkling of decent women but when it came to half past ten they all seemed to be attached. However, on a chance encounter with an associate from a nearby garage, while he was bringing me up to speed, he mentioned that he had got a new woman and was likely to bring her along to a small Auto-cross-cum-grass track event that I was organising in a spare field back at our farm. He happened to remark that he would probably turn up with her and her younger sister so he could leave the two of them chatting while he got on with some motor sport. The event was a low-key function with just about a dozen competitors having a run round a field. However, later in the day I came across my friend and his girlfriend, Eunice, and low and behold a younger sister called Valerie who, in the fading light, appeared to be reasonable. She certainly had a pleasant smile and looked to have a decent shape about her. There was obviously some sort of conspiracy between the three of them and so I was formally introduced.

I remember being encouraged to "give my sister a ride round in your Rally car." Being keen on this sort of thing I was quick to oblige; and the ice was broken. My self-confidence was always high at these functions and I managed to start a conversation. Her sister Eunice was quite intelligent and worldly wise; I know this because she told me so! Nevertheless I managed to have enough courage to ask Valerie if she would like to go for a Chinese meal sometime, which would be when I could get the next night off. I cannot remember how soon this occurred but I certainly looked forward to getting out for a night again and we seemed to get on really well. In any case it had been so long that I was effectively starting again.

After the first night out I took her back home to Chester-le-Street and was immediately introduced to her mother and father who made me feel really welcome. They were so interested in what I did and what I was busy achieving that it made me quite comfortable. Her father was a miner in the true North East tradition. He looked like a miner and acted like a miner, and was so proud of being a miner. Her mother had spent her life looking after him and Valerie's sister and two older brothers. I was delighted to discover that her older brother was involved and owned a small haulage business, which was a strong point of identification for me. At the time, Valerie was training to be a nurse. This was handy in some ways because she did a whole variety of shifts and while this would normally have presented a problem, we were often both off during the day and both working at night. Surprisingly, she quite fitted in to my way of life. We liked doing interesting things, going to interesting places and things. A genuine friendship, built on a good foundation, developed over the coming months.

While I certainly knew my way around a pair of knickers I still hadn't had an opportunity to break my duck. The coming months developed into a learning curve as we blundered along and learned together. I discovered some things in life are very skilful and take a long time to learn, like spray painting a car; it's a long time before you can get rid of the runs and come up with a good finish.

Even though Valerie had been at the farm on our first meeting, it was some weeks before she made an official return to meet my parents and sister. In many ways she took to the farm because she was so very fond of animals but was taken aback at times by the primitiveness of some of the surroundings. I remember when she was first inspecting the outside toilet, which was an earth closet. She was mumbling about there being no lock on the door, my father quickly pointed out that the farm had been in the family for two generations and no-one had ever stolen a shovel-full so she had no cause for concern. He then alerted her further that she couldn't use the facility on a Thursday morning as that was when the Council came and emptied it with two large hand shovels.

After our first encounter, which was in fading light, I realised with the sun behind her and on a clear day she had a fair good body shape and decent legs. I therefore was more than impressed when she informed me that she had purchased a mini skirt, which was the height of fashion. So when she turned up at work I was well impressed, then my spirits dropped as I realised that a mini skirt needed to be worn with this new fangled system called tights which, apart from being a bit of a nuisance, looked a bit unhealthy to me. So my aim in life was to convince her she would be better off, for the good of her health and my well-being, to stick to the somewhat longer skirt and the well-tried system of stockings and suspenders which as far as I was concerned had kept women in good health since the Second World War. I later found out that some tights were available with a reinforced gusset. No wonder there was so much absenteeism in the work place.

We would probably see each other about two or three times a week which I suppose was fairly normal in the 60s and after getting engaged we finally got married at Chester-le-Street in the Parish church. Though modest in size the wedding was a very good day. My father got well scrubbed up and got his new Trilby hat out and my mother was full of herself. My best man was my current co-driver, John Lee, and my side of the congregation was made up with a few friends from the Motor Club and from work. After the formalities and a good time by all we left for a honeymoon at Aviemore in Scotland but not before my vehicle had been tampered with. It had been daubed with lipstick and had the mandatory array of tin cans. I managed to get rid of the tin cans as soon as we got round the first corner but some of the other marks took weeks to get off.

The vehicle I was using was the only one I possessed. It was a Ford Escort 1300GT which was also my current Rally car, the one that I had won the North East Rally Championship for the first time in 1968. So after all the gala of the wedding the car returned to normal use but not before one ironic twist. While taking part in a rally some two weeks later we suffered a clutch problem and at the halfway halt I had to remove the sump guard, a thick aluminium shield protecting the engine and gearbox, to effect repairs. Imagine my surprise when the sump guard dropped to the ground and out fell three or four kippers. As I'd left the wedding reception they'd been placed on top of the engine but must have curled up with the heat and rolled down on to the sump shield because they were already well cooked and well preserved. I didn't pass comment, just left the fish on the car park floor for spectators to ponder over. There were several theories as to which river crossing we had traversed on the event and how we might have gathered them up as we passed. It was also interesting to note that most people seemed to think they were trout.

As we approached the wedding day our house purchase fell through completely and the only option remaining was living in a cottage at the end of the main farmhouse. It had been occupied for 15 years previously by my grandparents but had remained unoccupied for the last two or three years. I have to say that I enjoyed remaining on the farm but it didn't suit Valerie. She didn't like the travelling and she didn't like the lack of central heating and some of the other amenities but by and large she sort of settled in to country life. I remember her asking my father about the Christmas geese and why some of them were much smaller than others. He just replied as he walked away that the small ones must have been planted too deep and too far apart.

After a few months we managed to secure a good quality semi-detached house not far from Ansa Motors and within walking distance to work, in what turned out to be a fairly good area, but by the time we had carried out some mandatory work to get a dreaded mortgage and had moved in we were left almost penniless and effectively started life again. I remember Valerie's mother handing her five pounds to get something to eat, which was extremely welcome. However, with both of us working it didn't take long to get going again.

Not long after we were married and settled my uncle George, who was my father's identical twin, became quite ill and while visiting him in hospital he constantly referred to Valerie as "Joyce". So on leaving the hospital we jokingly referred to her as Joyce, so each time we re-visited and the Joyce name was re-instated; it provided us all with some good entertainment. When we tried to correct George he would have none of it and even when he left hospital and continued to live for at least another 15 years, he still knew her as Joyce and after that she simply was referred to as Joyce by all of us and has been ever since. Often now the only people who call her Valerie are those who haven't seen her for 20 years.

# CHAPTER VI

It may be different now but in past times, no matter who you were, when your vehicle decided enough was enough and let you down there was no other option but to stop, get out and hope that a passing motorist would offer assistance. I therefore came into contact with people from all walks of life. Many were successful professional people, but working mostly at night sometimes these unfortunate motorists were from the world of show business, radio and television. One of the first celebrities I encountered was Mike Neville who has been a Television News personality in the North East for 40 years. At that time he was doing a presentation at a local radio station titled 'Radio Durham'. Mike, at the time, was driving a Ford Capri which had experienced dynamo problems, so while I removed the dynamo and fitted new brushes he kept me constantly entertained with a whole series of stories and anecdotes of his past few years.

Over the years Mike must have dealt with thousands of people but when I saw him recently and reminded him of the occasion he clearly remembered the breakdown. He is no exception because any time someone is involved in a major breakdown they remember every detail just like when they turn up at the Casualty Department following some sort of accident. It is a piece of personal history etched on their brain whether they like it or not.

Radio Durham was one of several early local broadcasting centres set up by the BBC and basically surviving on local content. Now and again I came into contact with the news reporters as they attended various road traffic accidents but the other source of contact with these reporters was the more common one of breaking down and skidding into things. They were all young, highflying personalities who would go far in the world. One frequent casualty of bad mechanical reliability was Kate Adie who ran an old Hillman Imp. Even a good Hillman Imp was bad news and hers was no exception. I recall her being very tall and slim and a little bit unsuited for travelling in such a small vehicle. Apart from breaking down frequently she would often call at the workshop to ask if her vehicle was safe for a particular journey, which was probably less than 10 miles.

When dealing with these people I was totally unfazed and always believed, rightly or wrongly, that I was the one with the skills. After all, it was they who had come to me, either accidentally or by choice. Another news reporter, in fact I believe he was Head of News and Current Affairs at Radio Durham and he may also have been Kate Adie's boss, was Mike Hollingsworth who enjoyed his motoring courtesy of a Morris 1100. This was one of the most comfortable cars of its day but not very reliable and when it got a year or two older went very, very rusty. Mike's car was going through all these phases during his time at Radio Durham. He later moved to work for BBC Television in London and was kind enough to let me stay with him when I visited the capital. Perhaps he became best known nationally when he married Anne Diamond, herself a breakfast television personality.

Another regular breakdown customer was Charlotte Allan, a Tyne Tees television presenter, who was frightfully extrovert. Even when she hardly knew me, as I arrived at her broken down Volvo P1800S (which was the same model as that made famous by Simon Templar in 'The Saint'), Charlotte would run towards me in a great embrace, which was always embarrassing. If I wasn't in an oily donkey jacket I was certainly in a greasy boiler suit, but she didn't seem to care as long as I managed to get her car going. However, I still used to feel embarrassed if anybody was watching, but apparently this is how most show business types seem to function. In this tight-knit community, Charlotte's husband Chris, who also worked for Radio Durham, travelled around in a VW Beetle.

In the 1960's many pop groups travelled the roads, especially on a Friday and Saturday night. Usually there would be five or six musicians crammed into a seriously over-loaded van with sleeping bags and every other survival aid. If these vans failed it was often a crisis because they always had to be somewhere yesterday, so we often just finished up by putting a rope on and towing them to their next gig, which was usually in Middlesbrough or Newcastle or, if we were lucky, the local venue which was the Top Hat Club at Spennymoor.

Most of the turns at the Top Hat would stay at a Bed and Breakfast establishment a few miles down the road in Croxdale and it was this location where we would normally have to go to sort the vehicle out. The number of stars that had car problems was too numerous to remember. Usually I was dealing with a vehicle with just a 'roady' present, but I do remember Kathy Kirby being full of hell and looking just as rough because her Beetle wouldn't start one Sunday morning. Like a lot of Beetles it had a problem with the starter motor and only needed a brisk tow with a rope before she was on her way. I thought she was a bit long in the leg to travel comfortably in a Beetle and as she went off down the road I thought, "Better her than me."

Often it would be a talking point at a shift change of a Sunday morning as to which famous person had broken down the previous night and what they had been like to deal with. It perhaps explains a lot about people's outlook on life. I always found these high profile personalities very pleasant to deal with and all good humoured, whereas other members of the breakdown staff, Albert in particular, used to resent them and disliked everything to do with them. I never saw any of his customers to ask what they thought of him. Dealing with people who are broken down is by and large about having the right attitude but often these people are in such a stressful situation that they can make life unduly difficult for an unsuspecting breakdown mechanic and as time went by my attitude hardened considerably.

The cause of the problem was that often people would arrive at the workshop bemoaning that their vehicle had broken down several miles away. They'd got a lift, which was the expected and normal method because there were not many telephones and no mobile communications. When these people came across the forecourt towards the workshop my brain would go into overdrive to assess what type of character I was about to endure. Could I see a bulge in his pocket where he was carrying a full wallet; was he staggering slightly which might suggest that he had had too much to drink; was he dressed in a sensible and straightforward manner that would help to determine his character; was he a workman; perhaps his broken down vehicle was a 24-ton lorry carrying wet fish; or had he bought a brand new Corsair two days ago which had now let him down?

All these things had to be double guessed before he had even opened his mouth. Then once he started to talk, did he have a foreign accent or was he from Scotland, as was often the case. Rightly or wrongly, all these things had to be considered especially if it was 3 o'clock in the morning. Did he even have a car at all; was he just looking for somewhere to doss down for an hour or two? If that was not enough, what if in the half-light the person came into view and was in high heels and a skirt? If he had a foreign accent I would get concerned, even frightened, by his persistent and demanding attitude and a reluctance to pay for anything. Sometimes I would fear for my safety. I believe you can now get tablets to allay fear of foreigners. Sometimes my concerns would turn to a sigh of relief when one of these undesirable people, for one reason or another, would merely ask if we had a taxi. I would then quickly send them round to the filling station and the problem would become Colin P.'s. However, I would sometimes find that if things didn't go according to plan I would finish up with sore ears courtesy of Colin P. the following night.

It is easy to see, after having this situation arise week in and week out, that at other times it is easy to imagine that when an ordinary person who was broken down 200 yards away came on to the forecourt, they would wonder what sort of business they were approaching. It was interesting to see the situation from the other side of the fence. One year when Wislon and I were travelling to the British Grand Prix we encountered clutch problems near Newark and were faced with walking a few hundred yards to a nearby breakdown service. We stood outside the edge of the compound trying to decide the best attitude to adopt in order to receive the best possible service. It took us three or four minutes before we decided that only one of us should walk towards the attendant being sure to expose a broad grin and just happen to be carrying a wallet in one hand so he could see that we were serious. On that occasion we did receive the assistance that we were seeking, so we had got it right.

Now, when I look back, I realise it was the deceit of some people who made us the way we were, we didn't deliberately manufacture the attitude that we adopted. On one occasion someone who turned out to be too drunk to even find his car again had approached us. We'd got into the truck, gone down the road and wasted 40 minutes looking for his vehicle. He then said, "It's OK." and jumped out. He'd probably had a free lift home. We've asked people if they had money, they have shown us money but when we'd repaired the car, money seemed to disappear. We had people who would tell us they had a small vehicle, which had dropped into a small ditch; we quoted a price for such a recovery only to find on arrival it was a 5-ton bus down a ravine. And so the saga went on.

One of the most trying aspects of running an emergency breakdown service, since everything is always a stress purchase and a panic purchase at that, is getting paid. We all learned a long time ago that an offer to pay later, or for a bill to be sent would, nineteen times out of twenty, result in the loss of any revenue. We therefore developed a hard-and-fast rule: no money, no service. But as I have to keep reminding myself, we would often get caught out and having done the job we would likely not get paid. We always looked for some form of security or deposit, a spare wheel, worth about four or five pounds at the time was usually a good bet, provided it was not equipped with a punctured slick tyre. Occasionally a car was equipped with a radio, which would often help to get the customer back with some money, but usually we had to take a wristwatch, or something of sentimental value or so we thought. The attitude of people presented with this scenario varied enormously. Some would leave anything at all just to be able to go home, get some cash and return as soon as possible, so pleased that we had provided a service and so embarrassed that they were caught wanting.

One such job, when asked what he had of value, said, "Just this new suit that I am wearing for the first time today and if you give me a couple of minutes I'll put it on a coat hanger in its plastic bag and I'll be back within two hours." He happily drove off down the road wearing just his underpants and shirt, seeing the funny side more than we did.

Often, all we were doing was inconveniencing people. What could we do with a spare wheel from a 10-year old Ford Consul, or a wristwatch or bracelet that was supposed to be of great sentimental value? We even featured in a newspaper article with a photograph showing us standing over a table loaded with hundreds of items that had remained unclaimed. Sometimes people would turn up 18 months later, by which time we had thrown all the stuff in the bin. I never once felt that we treated a customer in any way other than how they deserved. 97% of people were treated like every customer deserves to be treated and these people responded to us like knights of the road, which is what we were.

An example of how we would not be messed about by a customer occurred one night. Stores Assistant John had been working overtime and was having a brew when a call came to attend a car some 10 miles south of Durham. A couple of minutes later I answered the telephone to a man identifying himself as Charles Lutterworth, he claimed to be a friend of the Managing Director. He was pleading for urgent assistance as he had broken down some two miles north of Durham in completely the opposite direction to the other job. When I explained that it would be 40 minutes he was almost in tears. He said that his car would have to be moved because it was broken down in a bad place and an accident would surely occur. I then turned the tables and said I would be with his vehicle in five minutes. I told him that the car would be towed back to the workshop where he would then have to wait until I had done the first job. Once again I emphasised the shortage of time.

John said he would ride with me as Wislon hadn't turned up. He was still busy with a Women's Institute General Meeting. When we arrived at the Ford Prefect, probably some six or seven minutes later, there was only a car and no driver. I was furious because I now saw a wasted journey or a long delay. So John suggested I shouldn't wait but just tow the car back to the garage. I decided that since cars didn't have steering locks there was only a door to defeat and I had already established myself as someone who could break into a car without damage in the time it took the owner to find the right key. Sometimes, if people were hesitant in coming out with a key, I would, almost like a party trick, open the car with a piece of wire, usually much to their amusement. After swiftly accessing the vehicle I placed John in the driving seat and connected a rope. The next thing I saw was a chap walking briskly but with a walking stick, after climbing over a fence some 15 or 20 yards behind the car. I indicated to John that we would nevertheless drive away because this chap had already upset me.

I then took the unusual step of taking the car forward at a speed that kept the man hoping he would be able to catch up with us and stop us driving away. A couple of times he even managed to tap the rear of the vehicle with his stick. I kept this up for two or three hundred yards until he ran out of energy and slumped onto the grass verge. We returned to the workshop with the vehicle, popped it inside and locked the door and went and did the other job. On our return, the first customer was sitting on the wall adjoining the workshop, still a little flushed in the face but full of his own importance. He explained to us in pompous detail how unfortunate he felt to have been so close but still failed to attract our attention. Mr Lutterworth complimented us on our diligence in towing his vehicle away so gently and smoothly. He'd even convinced himself that it was the rubber on the end of his stick that prevented us hearing him tapping the back bumper. He honestly thought we would have stopped.

Even Wislon fell foul of deception. One evening, just as he was about to leave for home, a rather plausible girl arrived on the forecourt. Going through our usual assessment we both summarised and agreed that she had probably missed her last bus, which she duly claimed to have done. The girl also told us that even if she had managed to get home she would have been locked out. She asked to spend the night in the workshop. Wislon, at this point, saw more than just a passing opportunity and offered the facility of his over-priced bedsit, which she immediately took up. I recall Wislon in all his haste had left without finishing his tea and set off home with this girl in tow, with me thinking "Lucky Wislon". The next morning, as I was leaving for home, I was stopped by a Police Officer who was on foot patrol. He asked if I had seen a girl called Susan who had escaped from the local Remand Centre by knocking over a guard and somehow climbing over the wall. She had been detained for stabbing an old woman in the local library. The description of Susan exactly matched Wislon's new-found companion but I thought, "The least said the better." so I said nothing. The following evening when Wislon came in with the fish and chips following a lengthy Council Meeting, he was somewhat distressed despite having been entertained the previous night. His companion had not only eaten his breakfast as well as hers but had stolen his watch before leaving without trace. We still felt 'the less said the better' and that was the end of the story.

# CHAPTER VII

There was always a fair amount of undercurrent activity between the male staff and some of the girls who worked at the filling station and one or two others who worked generally within the Company. However, in my position as an outsider it was difficult to keep track of what was happening. This was mainly because it was of no great interest as long as it didn't affect me. However, sometimes things would crop up that did concern me. It was one Monday morning at about quarter to eight when I arrived for work to begin one of my rare day shifts. Albert, who had been working the previous night, was still out on a job. I'd boiled the kettle and was enjoying a brew when someone came in to say that one of the filling station girls, Trudy, wanted to see me. I felt this was unusual as she usually didn't bother to speak to me. Trudy was carrying a parcel that was about a foot long and six inches square. She asked if I would be kind enough to give it to Albert when I saw him, emphasising that she didn't want anyone else to know. About half an hour later, Albert returned from the job he'd been doing and I offered him the parcel. I was surprised at his reluctance to accept it. Finally, when he opened the parcel we saw that it contained his left Wellington boot. He showed no surprise at the unusual contents of the package, it was as if he expected it.

Trudy's husband, who was a local baker, started work at 4.30a.m. so Albert would visit her half an hour later. On this particular morning her husband returned home to collect something he'd forgotten and Albert had to make a quick escape across the back garden. Heavy rain had turned the ground into a boggy mess and as he ran from the house

Albert felt his left Wellington boot being sucked from his leg. Because his escape was a matter of extreme urgency he had to leave it where it was, firmly stuck in the quagmire of Tracy's back garden. The whole story would have been quite funny if Albert had any sense of humour at all, but he just grunted. Then, without a word, he placed his left Wellington boot opposite the right one which he'd left standing in a corner of the canteen alone and unnoticed.

On another occasion a member of the workshop staff was suddenly dismissed. It struck me that Sir knew something that no one else did. When I asked why he had been dismissed I was just told that he was gone. I was therefore rather surprised to find that it might have been the result of something I'd said. The following night I received a call from a woman saying that she was broken down in Durham City. It would be around 2a.m. and I was not entirely happy but I suppose I'd become so sceptical of most things that it would have been strange for me not to be unhappy. I set out in an L/R only to find no trace of the broken down vehicle. It was not completely unknown for people to get started and do a runner but this situation was rare enough for me to be unsettled. My suspicions were further aroused when the same woman rang almost as soon as I had returned to the workshop. In an aggressive manner she complained that I hadn't provided a breakdown service.

I may not have been good with people, but I certainly was not stupid so I jumped into a car belonging to the Car Sales Department, grabbed somebody's different coloured jacket from the canteen and set off. I approached the supposed breakdown from a different direction. I was surprised to find Peggy, a girl out of the office, in company with the individual who had been sacked. I walked up behind their car, banged on the roof, then disappeared for self-preservation purposes. There were no further phone calls and I reported the matter to Sir the next day. I understand he tore a strip off the girl from the office. She denied ever having been there but, once again, he knew more about the case than I did, so he was in a better position to deal with it. I suppose if I hadn't taken the action that I did the deception could have lumbered on night after night.

Throughout the years that I worked for Ansa Motors I always found the Managing Director, Alan Able, absolutely amazing. Maybe I was biased towards my employer as I was when I worked for Alan Bromley, but I watched in awe at the way he dealt with each situation. The business with Peggy, the girl from the office, was just one of the many nonsense situations that he had to deal with. He was quiet spoken, very precise and always on top of the job. Although he was tall his mannerisms and preciseness could be matched in some ways to the style of Captain Mainwaring in 'Dad's Army'. The difference being, that instead of doing everything loud and wrong, he worked quietly, usually making the right decisions.

When we were doing heavy recovery jobs he often liked to get involved and this was the only area where I honestly thought he was useless. One day he attempted to supervise operations from a down wind position as the Fire Service hosed down an acid tanker on the Bowburn Interchange. Sir's face was red with the spray and I never saw that particular suit again, not even for gardening. Whatever he thought of me he never showed it, though I did get the job each New Year's Eve of transferring him and his friends to and from their social function. I always found it daunting. I was required to drive his brand new Jaguar, with all his wealthy business friends taunting me from the rear seat. Sir would sit in the front, having had perhaps only half a pint of lager. One thing is certain, he knew how to negotiate. On several occasions he talked me into doing jobs that at the beginning I had no intention of going anywhere near.

For example, I remember the time when there was a rear axle to change on a broken down heavy lorry. It was two days before Christmas and four feet of snow lay on the ground. Nobody in his right mind would have had anything to do with the job. Sir asked me why I wouldn't do the job. I listed about six reasons, including the fact that the temperature was below freezing, it wasn't my job, I didn't know anything about back axles on trucks and I had no tools that would fit the job. He replied by supplying a coke brazier with two hundred weight of coke, told me to take two men from the Commercial Department and if I needed any tools just to go out and buy them. Being a reasonable sort of person I was left with no other option than to get the job done. Working day and night on the side of the A19 the job took two days to complete. When it was finished I had a hundred weight of coke left over for my own fire at home. Sir finished up with the brazier for burning garden rubbish.

Sir's best skill was dealing with complaining customers. By the time he had finished they were so embarrassed they would be apologising to him. On one occasion the Humber 4x4 vehicle was being driven rather too hastily to the scene of a breakdown. As it crested a hill to go down the other side an unsuspecting motorist in a VX490 was overtaking a learner driver who had stopped to practice a hill start. The driver of the Humber braked sharply and stopped, as did the driver of the VX490, but unfortunately the ten-foot commercial tow pole positioned on the back and running over the cab, was launched like a torpedo. It speared through the windscreen, lodging in the empty passenger seat of the Vauxhall. The breakdown truck driver then put the pole back in position and suggested that the car driver had better return to speak with Sir.

Once the circumstances had been established, Sir spoke severely to the motorist. He pointed out that his manner of driving, overtaking on a hill as he had done, could have led to him being killed. He emphasised to the motorist that he owed his life to our driver who had the presence of mind to stop quickly. The launching of the tow pole should warn him how dangerous it was to overtake at any time. Eventually the motorist had had enough of being berated. He left saying that if he stayed any longer he would likely find himself locked up for some driving offence that he felt he had no part of.

I often watched as Sir explained to customers the problems with their vehicles. His explanation hinged on getting the maximum amount of business rather than finite technical details. I had already discovered that I could often diagnose the fault on a car by talking at length with the customer. It was often told that working with cars is like working with people. A doctor will first of all interview his patient to obtain a diagnosis. I would adopt the same technique, obviously talking to the car via the owner. Over the years I refined the skill to the nth degree working out that for almost every fault on a car there is a comparison to the way the human body works. In fact, many years later I would introduce to the roadside emergency service a team of people called 'Breakdown Doctors'.

Since cars began, people have often used terms like, "She's not running right." so the seeds were already sown. Besides, there was already a whole series of phrases that related to mechanical problems that had come from a human origin, like the term, "It's put a foot out." meaning a mechanical component had popped a hole in the engine. However, I felt there was much to be gained in explaining that the ignition system should be compared to the nervous system of a human, because it triggers all the actions; whereas, if an owner had oil pressure problems, it was easy to compare it with the way blood is pumped around the heart. This always helped to explain why there was oil on the dipstick but it was not being pumped around the engine. In other words the heart had stopped and now the brain was starved of lubrication.

The cooling system was best explained like a human when only one running temperature would do, too high a temperature and the engine is sick, too low a temperature and damage can occur. This is like an athlete not warning up before attempting a hundred yard sprint. And so it went on. The engine has to have just the right amount of air and oxygen and just the right amount of fuel. After all, a human cannot work right after too big a meal. It wasn't long before other staff started to pick up on some of my mannerisms. When one of the salesmen had a heart attack word got round that his oil pump had failed but we all knew what was wrong with him.

On another occasion we were discussing the likely outcome of a friend who was being treated for leukaemia. He was having a blood transfusion every ten days and we wondered how long he would last. One mechanic explained it was like having a head gasket gone on a car, which of course contaminates the oil. Instead of the owner repairing the head gasket he just keeps changing the oil and filter every week. We worked out that in time the engine would fail totally and that is exactly what happened to our chum.

It has not escaped my notice that many of these replacement joints that people are now fitted with have more than a passing resemblance to parts used in steering and suspensions. But of course the human ones are not yet as good as the car parts. Overall a Datsun can travel a hundred thousand miles over African roads and not need a single joint replacing. When replacement joints are fitted to a human they tend to wear out fairly quickly. Maybe it would help if, when fitting a knee or hip joint, the joint was equipped with a grease nipple to allow for perhaps two pumps of LM grease every ten thousand paces. The similarity here is that most mechanics claim that a prop shaft joint lasts five times as long if it is made with a grease nipple fitted and is greased, as against the sealed unit which is what the poor human has to put up with.

Although customers usually understood the similarity between a broken down car and the human body there was always the odd occasion when nothing would work. I innocently arrived at a Triumph 2000 that had stopped unexpectedly on the A1. I was greeted by one of those husband-and-wife outfits where the husband started the sentence and the wife finished it, whether it was the wife's end that he wanted or not. So when I asked what the problem was, instead of getting a straightforward reply I received a five-minute outburst. This was started by the driver of the car and as he ran out of breath his wife took over, he then resumed, allowing her to get a second wind and the reply went as follows. "I'll tell you what is wrong; I should not have bought this car. We've only had it three months and the last one was no trouble, in fact, my mother travelled happily in the last car. In all we had three family holidays. Before that we had a Ford Consul 375 Lowline, which was also a very good car. In fact we learned both of our sons to drive on the Ford Consul."

At which point I interrupted to say, "But what's happened to this car?" I then received a burst of abuse from the wife who laid into me saying, "The problem with you lad is you never listen. If you listened to people's problems you would understand the car better." She then continued to explain how they had travelled round the North of Scotland in the Ford Consul and two years later gone to Devon and Cornwall in the next car. They both could not understand why the present vehicle had stopped three-quarters of a mile from where they lived. I had a further three or four minutes of family history before they finally let me under the bonnet. It didn't take long to recognise that there was a shortage of fuel. Continued investigations revealed that the shortage of fuel at the carburettor was because there was none in the tank.

I then had a further non-technical explanation from the wife who recognised that the fuel gauge was on the low side of red but insisted that with the fuel gauge in this position the car should have travelled at least another four miles. I eventually extracted four shillings and eight pence for a gallon of petrol, tipped it into the tank and bled it through. Even though the vehicle then started, they were not convinced that it had cured the fault and we started to go back to how many miles the Ford Consul would cover with the fuel gauge on red. They were reluctant to pay for the breakdown service and felt on this occasion it would have been better if someone had come to their assistance who not only knew about cars but was also prepared to listen for ever to their family motoring history with all its woes.

Despite the best will in the world and the best intentions I did not always come out on top or win the day, like the time I was called to a

Zephyr-4, which had lost its electrics on the A1. It was obvious before I attended that a charging system had failed. The vehicle and two people had to be towed back to the workshop where the Zephyr would need a new dynamo. Before starting the job I established that the couple did not have enough money to pay for both the breakdown service and the cost of a dynamo; the whole job was over eleven pounds ten shillings. The motorist spoke openly that his money was four miles away at home. Following the repair he offered his girlfriend as security until he returned to pay his bill. It was not the first time that we'd done this sort of thing; it was common to take wrist watches and other valuables, so I was fairly comfortable knowing that I had a live person.

I was busy so I had not had time to engage the man's girlfriend in any conversation. She'd made herself a cup of tea and was sitting in my canteen area. However, after some 30 or 40 minutes our intrepid customer had not returned. I thought it was time to check my 'bond'. I started by asking her exactly where they lived and how long they had been together. I was completely taken aback when she said, "I've known him since he picked me up at the last roundabout as I'm hitchhiking to London. He just asked me to wait while he went to get money and this is why I'm waiting." After another hour I had to admit defeat, never to see the motorist or the Zephyr again and of course there was not much I could do with the security he'd left, or at least nothing that she would agree to. So she had to be released back on to the A1 to thumb another lift, obviously with a more reliable car, leaving me to explain to Sir how I had done a job for nothing and that somebody had got one over me.

While it was easy to lose patience with this sort of situation, it was just as frustrating when owners of broken down cars, in trying to be as helpful, were so thick and difficult that nobody was going anywhere. Some people just liked to have you disturbed at the most awkward time. I always tried to get home for Christmas dinner feeling that if a turkey had allowed itself to be stuffed and cooked the least you could do was to have the decency to eat it. Just as I was tucking in to a piece of breast I received a call at home to say that someone was ringing from a call box in Durham City and their vehicle was a short distance away. Something didn't sound right. Eventually, with half my dinner in one hand I collected this character. He hadn't visited a barber for a while and hadn't bothered to make use of a razor blade either. We set off towards his vehicle, which he described as being a couple of miles up the road towards Newcastle.

He bored me rigid with his explanation of how he had had to abandon his Mini Traveller the previous night, which was Christmas Eve, after it had run out of fuel. We continued and continued, as he kept assuring me that it would soon some into sight. After we'd covered about 20 miles we were in the middle of Newcastle. He then adjusted his story. The previous night he thought he was being followed by a police car and knowing he was clearly under the influence of drink had turned quickly into a side street and continued until colliding with some bollards that were blocking the end off, breaking among other things his distributor cap. He then did a runner before somebody reported him. So what he was now requesting was an accident recovery. I was not amused, but having gone this far I elected to continue. We started by going to the nightclub where he'd got drunk and worked our way supposedly back towards Durham, checking each side street and cul-de-sac as we went but there was no sign of his vehicle. He wanted to stay at Newcastle and search for it himself but I felt he had started from Durham and that was where he should return. Some months later he was involved in another accident in Durham. He insisted on explaining to me that his vehicle at Christmas had not been in Newcastle it had been in Gateshead some four miles away. On this occasion he was not going anywhere and we adjusted the charge appropriately to pay for the energy I had wasted over Christmas.

*The author, aged 4 experiencing his first taste of horsepower aboard Jack under the guidance of father.*

*The author, aged 18 enjoying his cricket*

*Bromley's Garage complete with Wolsley. 1961*

*The author opens his own garage and workshop. January 1973*

*Fred Henderson Team Toyota factory driver 1976*

*First attempt at the RAC Rally. 1970*

*The author, full of smiles, having just purchased a van from a pig farmer. Later transferred many people to the Newcastle dances. 1963*

*A typical overturned car right outside Ansa Motors headquarters, Neville's Cross junction. 1966*

*The author's very own first recovery vehicle. A Landrover 4 Harvey Frost crane. 1973*

*Second attempt in all the snow. 1971*

*RAC Rally and finally sorted to perfection. 1972*

*A typical heavy goods RTA. Plenty of contraband spread about. 1966*

*Hi-Mac rescued by Diamond T. 1967*

*Local housewives protest the constant presence of the Diamond T, fortunately to no effect*

*The Stanhope coach resting peacefully after giving up 17 bodies.*

*The remains of the Stanhope coach.*

*Scammell in all her glory 1970*

# CHAPTER VIII

During the 1960s, apart from the freeze of '63, the weather pattern had been fairly stable but there was one Saturday evening when it had been raining quite heavily from the previous lunchtime. As I began my shift nothing seemed unusual. Each time the phone rang it was just about another vehicle that had stopped in a puddle of water. It would be just a matter of driving to the scene, drying the ignition system and bringing the vehicle back to life. The rain continued right through the night, which meant that I didn't have much opportunity to sleep. On arriving home I went to bed, staying there for the rest of the day. I awoke just after 4 o'clock when it was still raining heavily. Starting out for work I noticed standing water had appeared on the roadside and several fields were already flooded.

Awaiting me was a backlog of stranded motorists so Albert stayed on duty for a few more hours and the two of us did as many jobs as possible. The rain became heavier and heavier. At 9 o'clock Albert went home leaving me on my own. Wislon hadn't turned out and there were places where the roads were flooded to over a foot deep. I took the decision to park up the Land Rover and transfer my tools and equipment to a Second World War Humber 4 x 4. This was a vehicle that stood fairly tall off the ground which I thought would be more suitable for the deep water. Being an ex-Army vehicle it also had a fully sealed ignition system that, in theory, should have allowed the whole vehicle to go under water since the air intake was high up above the windscreen. This capacity was something I had no intention of testing. A large petrol engine fed from two 20-gallon tanks powered this ugly duckling of a vehicle. The problem was that someone always helped themselves to the contents. An expensive refill had to take place before the truck could go anywhere, so it was little used. This made the vehicle miserable to use at the best of times. On this night, before I'd even started work, inside the driver's cab was soaking wet. It had no heater and no automatic demisting system, so the dampness became worse. I was rather pleased when I didn't have to use it for long that night.

By now it was almost midnight as I set off south down the A1. Some three miles later at a point where the River Wear travelled under the A1 I was astonished to find a wall of water some three or four feet deep across the road. While the River Wear normally flows some 30 feet under the road the river had broken its banks and had taken a shortcut over some fields and across the A1. It was impossible for even a big truck to traverse this piece of road, in fact not only was the water fast flowing and deep but every conceivable piece of debris was also travelling with the water. I noticed doors from what appeared to be old sheds. There were pieces of furniture and quantities of timber being swept along by the current. As I stood there, with only the headlights lighting up this fast flowing fury, I watched as an Armitage Shanks toilet cistern went past. I later discovered that I was seeing the remains of the village of Page Bank some five miles upstream where the contents of approximately two dozen houses had been completely swept away.

My main concern was to attend the broken down motorist two miles further on so I doubled back and tried to take another road through the centre of Durham, heading out towards a small village called Shincliffe. However, I couldn't get much further because the road involved crossing over the River Wear that had gone over the road by at least four feet. In the moonlight I could see a glass-sided sports complex where the water had risen five or six feet up the glass, so I assume it was also five or six feet deep inside the building. I also recall seeing two or three inches of the canvas roof of an old Land Rover washed up against the side of the complex. Even though the police were milling about advising motorists not to attempt these roads, nobody needed any convincing because the water was so deep. There were very few people on the roads and there was little that I could do other than take a casual ride around just to see how bad it was in other places. I was not surprised to find that everywhere was virtually cut off and had it not been the early hours of the morning there would have been absolute chaos. I realised that the rain had stopped, it had probably been stopped for a while but nobody had really noticed. By seven o'clock the next morning the river level had dropped to a point where the roads were only flooded to a depth of about a foot. By this time the motorist whom I first set out to help had been left rather than forgotten. I had to assume that from his side of the river he would work out what had happened.

There were many cars that had become tangled in this floodwater but I went home for the rest of the day. When I returned I found the workshop and garage forecourt absolutely spilling over with cars damaged by floodwater. Not many motorists ventured out that following night but I was still kept busy recovering cars that had been left in low lying areas, cars that had been innocently parked on what would normally have been a safe place.

There have been heavy rains and flooding since that time but nothing that came anywhere near the amount of flood water that spilled over that one night. The village of Page Bank had been evacuated and was never re-inhabited since most of the assets probably finished up in the North Sea, 18 miles downstream.

Apart from the L/Rs and the ex-Army Humber, the other vehicle that some members of staff described as the flagship of the fleet, was a Second World War Diamond T. This vehicle had seen genuine activity during the Second World War as a tank transporter. It was the most gruesome vehicle to drive that I have ever encountered but they were used as a heavy recovery vehicle until the mid-1970s. The Diamond T was powered by a supposed 16-litre six-cylinder diesel engine that had a maximum engine speed of 1200 rpm and a maximum road speed of 20 miles per hour. Between starting and reaching top speed there was a possibility of using 12 forward gears, though in practice we just used two or three, probably 6th, 9th and 12th. The vehicle had six wheels and no power steering and it was left-hand drive. Its redeeming feature was a very large drum winch with a 50-ton winching capacity which was more than enough for any vehicle ever found on the public roads. In addition, someone had bolted on a Harvey Frost crane of the commercial variety with two large winding handles. Using these handles with suitable reduced gearing it was possible by turning the handle two or three thousand times to raise the front of a 20-ton truck by 12 inches – sometimes twice that height was required for a safe recovery.

Starting a Diamond T was never easy, we always had to use a tin of ether spray and a tin only lasted about eight starts. The engine would start first on one cylinder followed some 20 seconds later by a second cylinder and so on until after a minute and a half of trying, all cylinders were running. It then took several minutes for the smoke to clear and for sufficient air pressure to develop in order to drive away. Since the vehicle was manufactured before any safety requirements had to be incorporated it was possible, if careless, to drive before the air pressure had even started to build. There would then have been no way of stopping this 24-ton monster. The vehicle was about as un-roadworthy as a vehicle can be and still be in daily use. It had one headlight fitted and I recall using roadside paraffin lamps to provide the mandatory red lights to the rear. We never owned any paraffin lamps but there were always plenty on road works, so we just stopped and put an empty one down and picked up two full ones that were already lit. Sometimes just to get lighted ones I had to stop and exchange them. I often wonder what the various contractors thought about putting down their own lamps marked "Wimpey" at the start of the night and next morning finding two lamps with some other contractor's name on.

For the technically minded the braking system was single line air operated, which meant that the brake pedal was like an air tap and when opened, by pressing the pedal, air pressure rushed to all parts of the vehicle and activated the brake mechanism. On releasing the brake the air completely disappeared from the system and the brakes were released. Everything had to be planned ahead; if too many applications were made in rapid succession the system became empty and the brakes rendered useless. On one occasion, when returning from the Weardale area, one of the pipes became damaged by a loose drive shaft. My only option was to cut a softwood wedge from a nearby tree, push it into the broken pipe and bend the end over, build the air pressure back up and continue on three brakes. I did this with a 10-ton truck on tow, which also had no brakes. Although we all got on and worked with this monster we were in many ways an accident just waiting to happen. Fortunately it never caused any problems on that front.

There was one time when I rescued a British army vehicle. Skilled every day heavy recovery was not a widely available service, so as people drove along the A1 at Neville's Cross the sight of the Diamond T became etched in their minds. In later times, when such a need arose, they would call for the services of our monster irrespective of whether it was appropriate and suitable. We were often asked to move all sorts of objects, factory machinery being the most common but sometimes heavy furniture, in fact almost anything that presented a problem. I was not surprised to be called to a Hi-Mac excavating machine. This is a tracked vehicle with a jib and neck like a scorpion. The vehicle is normally used for digging deep drainage trenches and was used a lot for burying cattle during the foot and mouth epidemic of 1967.

This particular vehicle, while attempting to construct a sewerage system connected with the new Durham Police headquarters had fallen on its sword, so to speak. After completing a rather deep and neat trench it succeeded in falling in and became completely jammed. I inspected the scene and decided we would not be able to remove this digging machine with our Diamond T. Eventually the Army was called and became involved but before long the Army had also fallen in the trench and we were returned to the scene. Though I was not personally involved this time, the Diamond T was used successfully to recover the British army vehicle and then the two units working side by side eventually recovered the Hi-Mac. Since the whole episode was quite near the centre of Durham it attracted considerable interest and several good photographs of the action appeared in local newspapers.

The most arduous task that I ever undertook with this already 30-year old vehicle was to tow a lorry, complete with valuable load, from Durham to London at a round trip distance of 550 miles at a running speed of 18 miles per hour. If that wasn't all, because of the design of the broken down vehicle we had no other option, or so we thought, but to tow the entire outward journey by connecting the two vehicles with a chain. When Sir asked me if I would do it, the prospect of travelling to London overruled my better judgement and I agreed to get on with the job. The lorry driver had long since gone home and my assistant was a new breakdown mechanic called Anthony who had transferred from the workshop to do day shift. However, he soon got sick of the job, leaving after just a few months. You either loved the job or you hated it, there was no in-between.

We left Durham after enjoying a stout Sunday lunch and decided that initially I would steer the broken down vehicle that still had its engine running to provide brakes and Anthony would drive the Diamond T. After two hours we would change over, which we did and continued to do so every two hours stopping only briefly from time to time to enjoy a pie and a drink until we eventually arrived at 5 a.m. on Monday in Putney in southwest London. By this time I was at the wheel of the lead vehicle trying to work from a sketched out map in one hand and a street map of London in the other. I was trying to drive smoothly so that Anthony did not have too much trouble keeping the chain taut. By good luck we arrived at our destination a bit the worse for wear but everything was intact. We turned round and headed back feeling that the sooner we got out of London the better.

The Diamond T might have been built for the Second World War but

I reckon there was more room in the cockpit of a Lancaster Bomber than in our recovery vehicle. There was only just room for two people, provided they were friends; there was no room to stretch and hardly any room to change position. Had it not been the middle of winter, I would probably have tried to sleep outside on the back of the vehicle. We just kept changing over driving and nodding off and then offering to drive again. I thought we had made good time coming back because by 6 o'clock at night we had reached Scotch Corner when the throttle linkage fell off. It didn't take long to repair the linkage but in doing so I noticed that we had never enjoyed anywhere near full throttle, not just on this London journey but also for the past three years! On giving the vehicle maximum throttle position we were able to reach 23 miles per hour. It didn't take us long to realise that if we had had maximum throttle all along, we would have been home in Durham before lunch on the Monday instead of 7 o'clock at night. We had no need to refuel because the vehicle carried 600 gallons of diesel, sufficient to cross the Sahara Desert. The Diamond T was hardly ever maintained because it was always felt that it would have to 'go the journey' being replaced by a more modern truck.

After its trip to London someone noticed that the Diamond T rear tyres, of which there were eight, no longer had a suitable amount of tread. They should have had about an inch on the blocks, but there was probably less than an eighth of an inch. Since the vehicle did not have many years left and new tyres, at least in the eyes of management, were considered a fortune, eight second hand units complete with wheels were obtained. This was courtesy of a trading colleague who dealt in supplying second hand army stuff. These tyres were almost new and were the genuine article but had been kept as spares during the Second World War. The price was about 10% of new. Everyone was excited by the bargain. The wheels were fitted and the vehicle parked up ready to go. Fortunately it didn't happen to me but the first person to drive the Diamond T with its new rear boots was full of himself, until he came to the first 90 degree corner some 300 yards from where he started. As the vehicle took the modest corner the 20 tons swayed to one side and all four tyres simultaneously burst, spewing sand everywhere. By the time he got the vehicle parked, two tyres on the other side had also burst. After 25 years of being parked in the army stores the tyres had perished from the inside out. All we could suggest was that these tyres must have been assembled and built up somewhere in the North African Desert. The only option was to roll the other wheels, which were fortunately still in stock, 300 yards to the stricken vehicle and refit all eight original wheels and tyres. As far as I recall the original tyres were never replaced again and the Diamond T saw out its days on what was left of this first set.

The Diamond T was always parked outside an 'Open All Hours' corner shop run by an Englishman who we always referred to as 'Dafty'. He modelled himself on Ronnie Barker in his 'Open All Hours' television programme and prided himself on having an uninspiring and stupid attitude. For example, he wouldn't serve anyone while he was watching the television Nine O'clock News in case he missed anything. He detested the amount of smoke the Diamond T gave off if it happened to be started up while his shop door was open. He would complain vociferously and even decided to ring the newspapers and complain about the health hazard. He thought the diesel fumes were tainting his meat pies, whereas we thought it made them taste better. However, his luck wasn't in because unknown to him, when he rang the Durham Advertiser, it was Wislon who answered the phone. Subsequently a very small article appeared about a shopkeeper who admired the Second World War vehicles and how he was amazed to hear one starting up at all hours.

Wislon had already, over a period of time, experienced the Diamond T himself. On one such occasion, which was late evening towards the end of a long hot summer, we travelled to a remote country lane. The intention was to winch a lorry loaded with grain sacks from a roadside ditch. As we went through the ritual of starting the vehicle there was a loud muffled explosion. The top had blown off the silencer which was about the size of a 45-gallon drum. It was directly under the passenger side floor and was causing an awful racket in the confined cockpit accompanied by lots of thick smoke of the type that was contaminating Dafty's pies. Wislon, who was not known for any mechanical genius, decided that if he lifted up the loose floor plate he could fill the hole in the silencer with an old donkey jacket he'd noticed lying on the back. This later turned out to be Albert's jacket that he'd mislaid for the last time. It muffled the sound and stopped the smoke and we set off the eight or nine miles to the stricken grain lorry.

As we got out into the country lanes and on to what was, in essence, a nasty gradient, considerable heat had built up in the shoulder of the donkey jacket, which was already covered in grease, resulting in it taking fire. The first I noticed of this was when Wislon started to cough, he could hardly breathe. We drew to a halt and he pulled the smoking jacket out of the cockpit floor and threw it out of the side door: we decided that continuing with the noise was the lesser of the two evils. We continued to the scene of the incident and quickly winched the lorry out of the soft ditch, we then had to travel a further two miles to turn round. As we turned, it was almost 10 o'clock and approaching nightfall, we could see the sky ahead was a bright orange, which was not unusual.

This, for many years, had been a feature of this part of the North East. The Consett Iron Foundry, some 20 miles away, always produced this effect when pouring iron ore. As we returned over the brow of the hill and started to descend, we realised that on this occasion it was not Consett Iron Works that was lighting the sky but Albert's donkey jacket that had burst into flame and set a whole hedgerow on fire. Some of the flames had already spread to a nearby wheat field. Wislon, using his superior level of education, decided that we should drive on and call at the next phone box to report the strange fire, which he did. Fortunately, not much damage was done. After about ten years the hedgerow grew back and only a small amount of cereal crop was lost. I do believe that burning the ground in this manner is actually good for it, but we were reluctant to claim credit.

There have been many break points in history where the motorist has had a sudden jolt. Having first to take a driving test was obviously a bit of a blow, the first 10-year MoT tests also turned out to be a nightmare for owners of cars like my original Standard Flying 8A. One of the landmarks that I recall was the introduction of the breathalyser test to establish whether a motorist had been drinking just before driving. 1966 had been a particularly busy year for road accidents; cars were starting to become quite brisk, seat belts and screen washers were an optional extra. People generally liked to specify screen washers when buying a new vehicle though they still thought of seat belts as being a bit petty, especially since most of them were quite difficult to use. So accidents, especially those involving drinking and driving, became very gruesome and the Government had to act.

Travelling the roads at night, as the job required, often led to coming across an overturned car with a couple of individuals standing surveying the scene. Quite often several people had arrived first and willing helpers would surround the incident. One November night as the frost was starting to settle the roads were very quiet and I was returning to base with Wislon on board. It was so late that I was intending to drop him straight to his bedsit. As we rounded a fast right-hand corner some five miles from home, we came across two cars that had collided head on and then veered away each one in its own direction. One car, obviously caught out with the white rind on the road, had crashed into the other in a substantial impact. It didn't look as if it had just happened, there was no smoke or steam and everything was still. Wislon remarked that it was rather a daft place to leave two vehicles.

We made our way past the cars, reducing speed only slightly and continued toward Durham. We pondered the situation and decided we should turn round and go back. It was only when we stopped and went to the first vehicle, a Vauxhall Victor that had totally disintegrated because of an onset of rust, that we realised there were two bodies still in the vehicle. They appeared to have been killed instantly and must have been there for more than just a few minutes. Wislon had made his way to the second vehicle, a Morris Oxford, which was parked on the grass at the side of the road. I could hear his voice and I assumed he was in conversation with somebody. He was however trying to establish whether the driver of this vehicle was still with the world. I ran over to where they where and realised that a middle-aged woman had been knocked unconscious and was busy trying to come round. We now had to try and get help. We were still using a mix and match half-cocked two-way radio system rented from a radio handling company. By the time we got through and explained the situation it would have been quicker to drive the two miles or so to the nearest phone box. Eventually the emergency services arrived and we were able to get away.

It once again reminded me how awful it must be to have any sort of road accident, particularly where injury is involved, with no help at hand. While we were at the scene, which must have been for half an hour, no other vehicle came along and there could easily have been two fatalities, which had turned to three. For all we knew the other two lives might have been saved if it had not been for the isolation. It crossed our minds that the accident could possibly have happened up to on hour before we came along.

The time leading up to the introduction of the breath test caused great speculation as to whether it would work fairly. Some people obviously thought they would be over the limit with just a sniff of ale. Others confidently predicted they could outwit the breath test because they were able to consume and conceal vast quantities of alcohol. However, despite the hype, I could not have anticipated what would happen on the first night of the new Regulation, which was a Sunday night. Motorists simply kept off the road, the highways were completely deserted and I did not do a single job. Even the truck drivers must have driven slowly, being rather concerned in many cases that they could fail this new fangled test just because they had earlier consumed a couple of biscuits that might contain yeast. There was no doubting the success of the legislation because Friday and Saturday night road accidents simply disappeared. It was a long time before I next came across an accident that was the result of drinking and driving. As time went by more and more people started to chance their arm but never again did we see the volume and despair that had been caused pre-breathalyser.

# CHAPTER IX

Over the years, each piece of legislation introduced to save life and limb (that couldn't be argued against) resulted in a further blow to the profit of our recovery service. The requirement to have 1mm of tread on car tyres certainly dealt a hefty blow. Previous to this legislation it was usual practice to run tyres down almost to the canvas. It would have been a blatant waste of money to remove a tyre that was other than bald. Of course a car with primitive suspension, poor brakes and a low ratio steering box was a perfect recipe for a decent road accident if it happened to rain after a few days of fine weather. I sometimes thought if more changes like the last two kept occurring we would soon have no road accidents at all!

I was still thoroughly enjoying my job, sometimes forgetting that the reason I had moved in the first place was to get more involved in Motor Sport. As a novice competitor I had been relatively successful with my GT-engined Ford Anglia. I had not been able to win a rally outright but had established my presence. One of the main problems was that I was hindered by my shift pattern. Although I was obsessed with competing I also enjoyed working overnight and especially at weekends, so I tailored my various activities around work. I particularly enjoyed taking part in Autotests which involved driving at speed around bollards placed around a car park. I found it relatively easy to win these events but they were usually low key. Another form of motor sport that fitted my work pattern was Autocross, which is a type of racing held in a grass field. A miniature racing circuit is laid out and cars would compete four at a time against the clock. Once again the Ford Anglia GT was an ideal vehicle and I often emerged victorious.

Although an Autocross meeting was held in higher esteem than an Autotest it was still a long way down the list of events that needed to be won. Recognition could never be achieved by just winning lesser events. One or two people had started to notice that I was slightly different from other competitors. One such person was a local engineer whom we always called 'JK'. He had designed and built the ultimate Autocross car. This was a vehicle, which from a distance looked like a circuit racing car. It was a single-seater where the driver sat in the centre. The engine, which had been taken from a Rover 3.5, was situated immediately behind the driver's shoulders. This, in turn, was mated to a Hewland gearbox, which had started life in a Formula One car.

While JK was one of the finest and most precise engineers not working in the motor trade, his driving was at journeyman pace. He was not immediately able to do justice to his thoroughbred. After a short test in one of Frank Jackson's fields, I used the vehicle at several Autocross meetings, sharing it with JK. It was amazing to drive a vehicle that had so much acceleration and traction but so little weight on the front wheels.

I won several successive events and established the vehicle as being well built and competitive. After various modifications and alterations the vehicle is still being used from time to time by JK. Since the competition has now reduced, it is still capable of getting an outright win despite its age.

Stock Car Racing was a popular, if rough and ready, pastime for a lot of people in the North East. There were three venues that were used on a rotating basis. One team owner asked me if I would like to drive a Formula Two stock car. The Formula One cars were absolute beasts usually being powered by about five litres of engine and weighing one and a half tons but the Formula Two variety was much more refined, being a miniature conversion and using only a 1300 cc engine. I took part in four or five meetings and managed to lead one or two races before stumbling for one reason or another. I never felt it was quite where I should be but I have to say it was an experience that I am pleased not to have missed, but it was a rally driver that I wanted to be and it was these events that I set my stall out to win.

I felt my driving career really started to take off when I was able to get hold of one of the first new model Escort 1300 GTs. Although this vehicle had a much smaller engine than my 105E Cortina-engined Anglia, the engine was much more efficient. The layout and balance of the Ford Escort was superb. Being built in a more modern manner, the body shell was also considerably lighter. I had plenty of time working overnight to prepare the vehicle and I recall winning a rally on almost its first outing. This was the year that we went on to win the North East Rally Championship.

I recall one particular rally that claimed to be the coldest and snowiest that had been run in the North East for 40 years. Temperatures plumbed to minus 20 (Fahrenheit, of course) and there was at least a foot of snow everywhere with drifting in many places. We started the rally seeded at about number five. It didn't take us long to overtake the other competitors who were struggling both with confidence and ill-prepared vehicles. When we arrived at the halfway fuel halt at about 2 a.m. we were so far ahead of everyone that some people thought we had retired and taken a shortcut when actually we'd covered the entire first half route. Of course, we could not re-start on the second half until the rally had regrouped; we then set off again at a gallop to arrive at the finish so far ahead that I was able to complete my full English breakfast before the next crew arrived. Unfortunately, there were so many problems for the organisers and so many sections cancelled and deleted that we did not win by the great amount that we should have done. But nevertheless we won, which was vital in those conditions.

At that time most types of motor rallies were run over Saturday nights, covering about 300 miles. If I was on the day shift roster I would finish work at 5 o'clock on the Saturday evening, have something to eat, arrive at the start of the event around 8 o'clock at night and drive through the night, then return to work for 8 o'clock the next morning. I would stumble through the day and finally get to sleep on the Sunday night. One feature to consider was that I could not afford to crash or break down during the rally or I might have been late for work. However, if my tour of duty involved a night shift, I had to do a very poor trade-off with Albert in order to get the night off. I would be working the Friday night when it was vital to get a few hours sleep, I would then have to do Albert's shift on the Saturday to enable him to do my Saturday overnight. He then needed Sunday off again so I would return from the event and have to continue to work until the following Monday morning. Sometimes it got a bit difficult but overall I developed the technique of sleeping 10 or 20 minutes as often as possible, at least until the phone rang. Eventually I felt I could go on forever so long as I managed to total three or four hours sleep every twelve hours. It was only in later years that I realised how much speed I must have lost when driving through lack of sleep, probably at least one second every mile, which probably added up to two or three hundred miles.

Despite this arduous schedule I still managed to win the North East Rally Championship for the first time in 1968. This was the premier championship in the whole of the North East and encompassed the four northern counties, Durham, Northumberland, Cumberland and Westmorland. Even though I won this championship I never felt overawed with the achievement, I just felt that it had to be done if I was going to progress.

# CHAPTER X

Primarily I was trained and developed as a car mechanic and most of my work involved disabled cars and light vans. Because Ansa Motors was very strong in the recovery of heavy vehicle casualties, we had to deal with the occasional broken down truck or bus. This was one aspect of the job that I didn't like, I didn't derive any satisfaction from sorting out broken down trucks. This was in contrast to Albert who was trained on heavies and didn't like cars. They were always very heavy and dirty to work on, not to mention some of the loads they were carrying. In the 1960s loads were not well contained and they always spilled over on to the mechanical parts. Some of the worst that I recall were trucks that carried old bones and carcasses. These vehicles could be detected two miles down wind and the contents tasted from a distance of a hundred yards. I was often offered a few bones for the dog from one of these carcass-carrying trucks, but that was an offer politely declined.

There were many lorries travelling overnight that carried wet fish. I believe these fish were salted which lead to loss of electrics to the rear lights and even corrosion to some of the truck components. Up until the early 1970s, unlike passenger cars, heavy goods vehicles did not require any form of MoT, so many of these vehicles just rotted away courtesy of the dripping cargo. Many times I had to replace a brake pipe just under the chassis and under the load and often at 3 o'clock in the morning. My donkey jacket would stink of fish for weeks. It was not hard to take a dislike to these jobs.

The drivers of some of these vehicles had to be admired, but certainly not envied. They would leave home on the Sunday night, returning the following Saturday evening, just driving and sleeping all week. If asked where he was staying the night or where his digs were a driver would indicate that he was staying in Commer or Foden House. On looking at his vehicle it was apparent it was a Commer Carrier 16-tonner, or maybe a Foden truck. Often these drivers, once restored to full mobility, were very grateful; after all they didn't have to pay the bill. They would, on many occasions, reward us with a handful of the load, but the only problem was that the packages were often on the large side.

However, these consignments of goods were more than welcome because I had recently found time to get married and had bought a small house within walking distance of the workshop. A welcome job was recovering a truck delivering goods on behalf of a Christmas catalogue. The truck had overturned into some trees spreading a load of assorted goodies everywhere. However, as the old saying goes, one man's meat is another man's poison. An expensive woollen rug may not be any use once one corner had been dipped in gear oil. Following numerous attempts at cleaning, it took a good eye to spot where the mark had been, though the original customer would not have accepted it. Many other items were similarly damaged. The truck was also carrying wallpaper and paint, together with some rolls of mural wall covering which had a very attractive Austrian alpine scene. Over the coming months many of the staff would redecorate their kitchens using this Austrian wall covering.

I have many memories of being given a tip by virtue of some of the load, which then lasted for years. Most trucks were just loaded in an *ad hoc* manner and a couple of bags would never be missed from 20 tonnes. Quite often the driver would indicate that he had an allowance of load for such occasions. Sometimes the nature of the load meant it was best to politely decline: I saw no need to take four stone of turnips. I didn't like the fish wagons though Albert was very keen on his wet fish, as was Winston, one of the regular night shift attendants in the filling station. They would share many a box but often the stuff would lose its freshness or go rotten before it could be consumed.

Another useful perk for the overnight staff, especially filling station attendants, was the decision of some Scottish and Newcastle tanker drivers to take their break at the nearby coffee machine. During previous weeks Albert had 'persuaded' these drivers to allow him to loosen the drain cock slightly on one of the tanks. Winston, using a cleaning bucket, would recover about a half a gallon as another two or three gallons spread over the road. After all, who would miss four pints out of five thousand gallons? This was spread around to whoever was present and provided a pleasant distraction on a long evening shift. Though not a real drinking person myself, I would often join in this frivolity. One of my fondest memories was obtaining a hundredweight sack of powdered potato mix, similar to Cadbury's Smash, the type with onion flavour added. It lasted me for years even though I kept handing out portions to anyone who called at the house.

Most truck drivers would go out of their way to be pleasant because, after all, their immediate prospects of going anywhere depended on us. Now and again we would come across somebody who just did not deserve to be helped. I always believe in the motto, "Do unto others as they would do to you, but do it first." On this occasion I was called to a medium sized lorry that had slipped into a deep ditch. It was carrying boxes of Cape apples. Because the company had not paid for the last recovery job we were not prepared to restore this current vehicle to the highway until both the last job and the current one had been paid for.

As it was after 6 o'clock at night there was no chance of any money changing hands before the next day. Also, in order to establish the cost of the second job, I had to make a visit to the scene, whereupon I was faced with a whole load of abuse from the driver. He would have to spend the night in his cab but informed me that regardless of what I was going to do, he would go to the pub until it closed. On the assumption that you get nothing if you don't ask, I enquired about the availability of a box of Cape apples. His response was such that you would have thought that I had asked for the full load and he disappeared into the dusk still ranting and raving. I spent a few minutes assessing the situation and costing the job and decided to avail myself of a box of apples in any case, which I took back to work and took home for the night.

A representative of the company had turned up with a pile of cash, having driven over a hundred miles. Being aware that the driver would be less than helpful I borrowed John from Bisley, we then set off. On arrival at the scene the driver, who had obviously benefited from a skin full of alcohol, was in very high spirits. He would, after all, soon be back on his way. We quickly restored the vehicle back to the highway and to my surprise the driver then called me across with the remark, "If you want a couple of boxes of apples feel free, because some sod has stolen a box while I was at the pub." He made it quite clear that had one box not gone he would not have parted with another three.

So at the end of the day I finished up with four large boxes of wonderful Cape apples which I was assured would keep because of the way they were packed. It wasn't long before, while sitting watching television at home, I noticed a yellow fluid starting to drip from the living room ceiling. This coincided with the recent arrival of a new dog that had not yet established a regular routine regarding housetraining. Jumping up, I went in search of the offending animal in order to take reprisals. However, on continuing with the investigations I realised that the apple stock had started to soften down. The ensuing quantities of juice had not only saturated the spare bedroom carpet but there was sufficient juice for it to have worked through the joists and down on to the ceiling. If I had been an expert in these matters I would have noticed that the pile of boxes had sunk to half the height, meaning that what started as four boxes of good quality apples finished up as a pile of rotten fruit which took a lot longer to remove from the house than it had taken me to remove the original truck from the ditch.

One truck driver for whom I had changed a punctured wheel said, "Get yourself a few sweets out of the back." When I looked over the tailgate of this 40-foot trailer it was three-parts full of Raspberry Ruffles, all in their little pink wrappers. It simply looked as if the truck had been loaded with a mechanical digger. I wrapped as many as I could inside my donkey jacket and when I got back to base I probably had a good bucketful. There were certainly more than enough to set in a good case of tooth decay.

Sometimes the drivers of these broken down trucks would have to sleep overnight until we could get spare parts. They usually crashed out at the other end of the canteen and were so glad for the comfortable surroundings having been driving for the last 36 hours. They were no trouble whatsoever. I have often known the phone to ring, I would take the call, go and do the job, return to the workshop, nod back off and the next morning the driver wouldn't realise that I had been in and out.

The perks that a successful breakdown operator received came not only from these truck drivers but from most motorists who, by courtesy of the AA and the RAC, had free service and they would often tip generously. I would average about £10 per week in tips, which was another 25% of my wages. Some of the bits and pieces that we acquired had to be treated like the Crown Jewels or the workshop staff would feel that some of it, if not all, was theirs. I quickly learned not to leave anything lying about, otherwise it would be gone. One not so wise relief breakdown operator had left a large box of fresh vegetables that had been given to him by a grateful market trader. However, the following night, when he got the box home, he found a selection of quality carrots, leeks and onions on the top of the box. Underneath was a load of old car parts, so most of the results of his hard night's work would be finishing up beside somebody else's roast beef and Yorkshire pudding.

Sometimes, when a heavy goods vehicle crashed or overturned, its load would often be referred to as 'wasted'. Sometimes the owners of the lorry would attempt to salvage as much of the load as they could. If the scattered cargo was, for example, building materials the task was relatively simple but if it was loose cargo or one of our famous wet fish wagons, there was never much that could be realistically recovered and sold on.

In later years I recall a lorry loaded with loose apples overturning on the newly opened Durham motorway when the carriageway had suddenly iced up one autumn morning. The coefficient of friction between a Granny Smith and an icy road surface is virtually zero. On the first spillage the fruit rolled hundreds of yards and they were further sped along with the passing traffic. It was not very long before there were apples over a mile and a half of carriageway. There was no way that this crop could be recovered and put on display in a local supermarket. Also on this occasion there didn't seem to be any great demand for passing motorists to stop and collect a pound or two. In other words, the entire 10-ton just got wasted and the remains went rotten by the roadside.

However, when an Esso fuel tanker overturned and fuel was running from every orifice, it was amazing how many different types of vessels came into play to save the fuel from being wasted. Even so, an enormous amount of waste would still take place. I made haste back to the workshop and collected as many suitable or unsuitable containers as possible but despite strenuous efforts I still only finished up with about 40 gallons, the other 2,960 must have just seeped away into the earth, which in reality was where it had come from in the first place, but of course not from the subsoil of a barley field at Ferryhill.

Recovering fuel tankers was always a chore, it was always assumed they might explode but if one had done, keeping 10 yards back rather than 10 feet would probably have made no difference. The broken down variety often had to be towed overnight when there was less traffic but, all in all, it was just part of the job. However, when connected to the rear of a Diamond T, there was quite a long train and sometimes we had to drive directly through the centre of Durham City where the streets are extremely narrow. Though it didn't seem like it at the time, there must have been very little room for manoeuvre.

Sometimes when the weather was bad and especially if it was snowing, clearing an overturned vehicle could be quite demanding. More often than not I was on my own, as was Albert when it was his shift. The whole job was tackled with as much professionalism as we could muster but compared to later years everything was very primitive.

Occasionally, loads were just completely lost, like the petrol. A lorry carrying white lime skidded and overturned in a snowdrift at 7 o'clock one winter's evening. It could be argued that the shade of white was different but it was impossible to do anything about it. By the next day the snow had started to melt which then washed the white lime down the road, so after a few days both the lime and the snow had disappeared. There was a company that seemed to specialise in carrying sawdust in what amounted to great big boxes with a tarpaulin over the top. So, when one blew over in a gale force wind and split open it was only a matter of half an hour before the 12 tons or so of sawdust had disappeared without trace. Once again Nature had put it back where it had come from.

Despite finding ourselves in odd situations and dealing with so many different functions, the job never felt dangerous. When I look back I don't remember any of us getting a scratch or a sprain, which seems a miracle in an environment where one or more of us could have been killed at least twice. However, I do recall one incident where I was only too well aware that I had had a narrow escape. It started about 4 o'clock one December night; it was raining and freezing cold. Driving the Diamond T I went to a job somewhere near Sunderland where a new-fangled device call a skip lorry was attempting to unload by tipping the contents of the skip into the sea. In a perfect world, as various trucks tipped their rubbish, the landfill site would extend out into the sea a bit at a time. On this occasion, in the dark and wet, the driver had reversed too far and his vehicle had slithered down the slope leaving the rear wheels in the sea and the tide coming in rapidly. I had set up anchor and attached a strong winch rope to the skip wagon. The whole operation was no problem for the Diamond T winch and the lorry started to make its way back up the almost vertical slope. However, as the stricken vehicle came slowly over the top and back on to a flat surface, the whole scene being lit by only a couple of hand-held torches, we realised that the empty skip was missing. It had fallen from the back of the truck and was laying half in the water and half in the rubbish, still the right way up.

The owner of the skip wagon started to become excited, pointing out that if we weren't quick we would lose the skip. So, dragging the winch rope and a couple of chains, we both set off back down to the skip. Even though it was still beached, the skip was some two or three feet from dry land and was presenting a challenge to get a chain attached. I had already become wet shod so with nothing to lose I waded out to attach the chains to the skip. In the almost pitch darkness I failed to notice the arrival of a somewhat larger wave, brought in by the rising tide, which lifted the skip at least two feet up in the air. Suddenly I had nothing under my feet. The only option was to launch headfirst into the skip. It all seemed to take just a few seconds but when I looked up I had moved some 10 or 12 feet from shore and was floating. I didn't even have a torch and I couldn't think how I was going to avoid being swept out to sea. Before I could recover my senses another big wave came and washed over the skip, completely soaking me. Fortunately it drove the skip back into the rubbish where two or three people had gathered to quickly get hold of the chain and attach the winch rope. I must say I was out of the skip and into the slurry like a bat out of hell. All that remained was for me to winch the skip back up the slope where the truck itself, which was undamaged, loaded its own skip. I must say the skip owner thanked me profusely for saving his skip and I believe he even rang Sir the next day to say how pleased he was.

But in the meantime I was absolutely soaked with dirty, salty water and was starting to freeze to death. As I drove back towards Durham I really did feel as if I was going to die of the cold. I believe as the wave came over me had I thought, "This water's not too cold." But now I just could not believe how cold it really was. The anxiety and concern for my own safety reminded me of when I had had to struggle home from the dentist, half bleeding to death. Then I was frightened of the unknown, this time I was just in so much discomfort that the cold was almost unbearable. It was not just the cold but also the extra weight. My donkey jacket pockets were full of water and combined with a boiler suit I must have been carrying about three gallons.

Eventually, after reaching base, I stripped off as much as I could and went straight home to get in a hot bath. Even that was painful because going from cold to hot is not such a good idea. But, like all these situations, once I got a change of clothing I was back to work and out on more jobs within the hour. I remember it took me almost a fortnight to get my donkey jacket dry; but it never was right, it had white bits all over and always smelt funny. It was then that I wondered exactly what the wagons had been tipping.

As far as I can recall no one ever openly stole anything from an overturned vehicle. This would have been totally unacceptable both to the integrity of our operation and of course a matter of pride to the recovery staff. Often the police liked to get in on the act. They would cajole the truck driver to see what was going spare, especially if a load fitted in to the domestic household as in the case of a small truck loaded with various puddings, both of the treacle sponge variety and also Christmas puddings. I was to discover that one of these delicacies fitted nicely into an upturned policeman's helmet. There was a continual chain of officers backwards and forwards with their helmets under their arms on the outward journey and on the top of their heads when heading back to the overturned truck. In fairness, these puddings would not have looked well on a shop counter with a flat on one side where they had skidded down the tarmac. I have it on good authority that they taste just as well with or without gravel rash provided of course they are properly prepared.

If the food was perishable it was more likely to be discarded. We were more likely to finish up with a share but, like the 8-stone sack of mashed potato, a side of beef or a full-size ham took a bit of handling. Only the expert scrounger could take advantage of such an article. I had the unique advantage of being able to take a side of ham back to my parents' farm where they knew how to salt and preserve it just as they had done years ago when I was small and we used to keep what we called a 'house pig', which was a pig that was killed and cured each autumn to feed the family over the following winter.

When Sir heard about this meat being available he called me into his plush office where, in a round about way, asked me where his share was. I managed to go the three miles back down the A1 where the vehicle had originally overturned to find him a suitable specimen from the ditch. I removed any traces of nettle and grass and told him where it was in the workshop. I'm not certain how he coped with it but it certainly disappeared.

Sometimes, with all the best will in the world and with all the best intentions, the whole situation can just backfire as once occurred when we had three and a half tons of sweets spread all over the notorious Silom Bank just west of Durham City. The story began as we arrived and the vehicle was lying on its side with the roof split open. Its load had been a complete range of confectionery that had been contained in numerous two-pound cardboard boxes. There were many different varieties of wine gum-type sweets including Jelly Babies and Jelly Tots, which were a form of assorted wine gums. There were also boxes of liquorice that were labelled 'Poor Bens'. The range and variety was everything that a small child would ever want.

However, many of the boxes were bruised, a few were split open and some had been crushed. A representative of the company arrived and declared the lot a total loss and instructed us to get a JCB and just take the whole load to a tip. He indicated that he didn't even want the few good boxes back. Sir had arrived on the scene as he often did on these higher profile jobs and decided that he would call for a couple of small vans where he would recover the best part of the load and make it available for charity. We then recovered the overturned vehicle, got the majority of the load removed to a safe tip and swept the ground clean, as we thought. As we returned to base Sir and his advisors were working on a plan to deliver a complete range of sweets to all the hospitals in the North East where there were children. So, by next day, a dozen or more hospitals had enough sweets to last them for the next five years and all seemed wonderful. However, as I was sitting at home watching the Ten O'clock News there was a news flash to say that upwards of eight youngsters had been admitted to hospital after eating sweets contaminated with brake fluid and battery acid. What it failed to explain was that these kids had become hunter-gatherers and had located Jelly Babies and Jelly Tots in the undergrowth near the crash site that we had missed or never thought anyone would look for or find.

The next day hospitals that had taken delivery of the sweets were on the phone. All the sweets, even though they were absolutely perfect, had to be collected. We were left with about two tons of high quality confectionery, which finished up being stored in the back of the car valeting area where they had lain for months, or so I thought. But life being what it is, one day I decided to go and inspect the stock and found only a sprinkling of Poor Bens left. It turned out that some enterprising member of staff had, over a period of months or even years, sold them on round the pubs in the North East of England, effectively turning them into beer money. He didn't have a car so the entire two tons had left the site, one box per day, in his 'bait bag' courtesy of local public transport. The way these sweets were moved reminded me of how the prisoners moved soil from a tunnel in the prisoner of war film 'The Great Escape'. I always felt it was ironical that but for a little bit more commonsense a better use could have been made of this wasted load.

# CHAPTER XI

While the Diamond T had been the backbone of the commercial vehicle recovery business, with impending legislation it was obvious that its days would be numbered, but not before it had been involved in one or two further incidents. In defence of myself and other people involved in accidents, it has to be said that the concept of the vehicle was designed to traverse deserts and open country where the only thing to collide with would be an inattentive camel.

One of my last jobs with the Diamond T was an unfortunate journey travelling some 40 miles and steering an ICI tanker while being towed by Albert after he had endured a 16-hour shift. One of the disadvantages of driving this horrible beast was that half the total length was taken up with a long and high bonnet, the top of the radiator was in excess of 10 feet from the ground and the driver sat in a low seat some 12 feet back. After dropping the tanker and starting our return journey we stopped at a set of traffic lights in the centre of Middlesbrough where it went completely unnoticed that an elderly lady in an Austin Seven had dropped back out of the line of sight and under the front. The lights were still on red when Albert dropped his cigarette on the cab floor. He was busily searching for it when the lights turned to green. Albert, who was still grovelling around the floor of the cab, had failed to notice this so it was left to me to notify him. The woman in the Austin Seven had also failed to notice the lights had changed, so as far as Albert was concerned an apparently clear road lay ahead for several hundred yards.

We lunged forward, collecting the Austin Seven as we went and continuing up the High Street with the vehicle and occupant scraping along under cover of the radiator and sump. The scale of the vehicle can be judged when motorists and pedestrians finally waved us to a standstill and I noticed that the large NATO specification tow-hook under the front of the vehicle had gone through the rear window. It was lodged between the shoulder blades of her nodding dog, which had been positioned on the back parcel shelf. The radiator drain cock had pierced the car roof. After a fair amount of backwards and forwarding we managed to separate the two vehicles and the distraught old dear managed to get out. Somehow we were able to convince her to take a taxi home where she would be able to enjoy a cup of tea with plenty of sugar, which would prevent the onset of any delayed shock.

In order to clear the road we manoeuvred ourselves into a position where we could hook the Austin Seven on to the back of the 24-ton Diamond T and we just brought it back to Durham. I was not party to how the situation was eventually sorted out but I noticed that any promotion within the company that Albert was due appeared to be put on hold.

A couple of days after the incident with the Austin Seven, Wislon had just arrived on site as I was cranking up the old beast. Once the smoke had cleared sufficiently we left the parking area and took a tight hairpin turn to go north. There was quite a bit of traffic, which was ducking and diving to get past the slow moving breakdown vehicle. We must have reached over 10 miles per hour and I was struggling with the gear selection because of the heavy cold gearbox oil and the lay out of the transmission. There was an unusual noise, which appeared as though a tooth had come off one of the transmission gears from the rear axle. I felt that a gear lever seemed to move. Looking at each other we both thought the same thing, "The sooner this vehicle was laid to rest the better."

With this in mind we increased speed and set off to attend a brewery wagon that had broken down near Newcastle. After about half and hour of travelling, by which time we had covered eight or nine miles, we were brought to a halt by a Police traffic car, an Austin Westminster 105 which was the traditional black in colour but had the doors painted white. We felt this should have been the forerunner to the Panda car but this was never to be. I was totally unconcerned at being flagged down; I was hoping that he was not going to ask me about some cigarettes or the like from a past job. I was therefore quite amazed as was Wislon when we were informed that we had been involved in a nasty accident. The unidentified noise that we had heard in the transmission was the aftershock of a red Mini absentmindedly ramming the back of our beloved breakdown truck.

As we sauntered round to the rear of the Diamond T it was only too apparent that something displaying red paint had indeed gone under the back, colliding with the rear differential and bruising the differential oil pan. Again, I noticed that the NATO specification tow-hook, this time the rear one, had picked up considerable paint. I later discovered that this had engaged the Mini on the top of the windscreen, which had allowed the driver to slide forward and make contact with the steering wheel and windscreen, leaving her slightly the worse for wear. Fortunately there were plenty of witnesses who were able to describe the inattentive manner in which she rode under the back of us, which ensured that no further action was taken. Certainly no action was required with regard to the Diamond T. I don't think we even wiped off the tartan red paint and we were certainly unable to remove the bruise from the diff. casing.

As the Diamond T appeared to get longer and longer in the tooth each job that we undertook, at least from my point of view, became more and more of a chore. We never knew what part was going to let us down next. It already had hardly any lights; in fact, it hardly had anything other than the big Hercules engine. I was not surprised when I was winching a 24-ton sand lorry out of an escape road on what was known as Newton Cap Bank near Bishop Auckland when a non-mechanical housewife came out of one of the adjoining terraced houses. She drew my attention to some white-hot nuts and bits of bolts that were dropping down under the vehicle and setting fire to the tarmac. I could hear the winch grunting and groaning as it struggled on the steep gradient but it had always grunted and groaned and creaked as well sometimes, but why it had suddenly decided to lay hot nuts and bolts I wasn't sure. Each nut was at least an inch across the flats and with the broken bits of bolt there must have been six or seven bits and still the winch continued and the sand wagon slowly was pulled from its trap. More than 20 or 30 minutes must have passed before I moved the Diamond T clear, whereon the still hot bits of metal had sunk into the tarmac road surface. To my amazement the woman who had notified me was standing nearby and said, "You'll need these, son." She handed me a pair of fire tongs, no doubt part of a set of fire tongs, brush and shovel, which would be set beside her coal fire. Not wanting to show dissent I carefully lifted the remains of the nuts out of the hot bitumen and threw them into the grass on the opposite side of the road.

When the job was all finished and the vehicle was parked back up outside Dafty's shop, I started to investigate where these bits might have come from. I could not find any trace of any parts missing. I even had other members of staff looking for bolts that were missing but we found absolutely no trace and could not account for what must have happened. Fortunately, time was running out for this vehicle so the mystery had to remain.

This was just about the last job that the Diamond T was to do. It was to be replaced by a more modern Scammel Constructor, which was a heavy locomotive-type tractor vehicle that had formerly been owned by Pickfords, a large international heavy haulage company. I had selected this vehicle after a trip down south with Sir and felt flattered to be asked to assist in the specification. He agreed to all the modifications and equipment that I asked for but just before the new vehicle arrived I had enough time to knock down a telegraph pole and light tower with the old Diamond T. Its steering had become so stiff and difficult I was not able to take a slight roundabout without disaster.

I was more than delighted to see the back of the damned thing. As it was taken away in part exchange the only destination I could thing of would be a museum. A new era dawned. When we lost the Diamond T we lost an old man, stubborn but full of character. When the Scammel arrived we got a bright new executive, fully functional, brilliant brakes, power steering, it even had windscreen wipers and washers and a nice big cab with a heater. It was wonderful to drive and use but it was very plain in personality and compared with the Diamond T it was not very powerful. However, we had only had the vehicle just over a week when a job was to arise that would test man and machine to the full and also get the attention of the whole of the North East of England.

As I arrived to start my normal evening shift nothing seemed out of the ordinary, it was one of those wonderful, peaceful late summer evenings. By around half past seven I had completed two routine jobs, both involving the remobilising of broken down cars. I had returned to base via the local chip shop and was busy tucking into my fish and chip supper, a shade earlier than I would normally do. The air had been considerably freshened with a quick shower of rain that had also highlighted the pleasant aroma of the nearby grass verges that had been cut that day by the local Council. I had taken up position on the low wall at the edge of the garage forecourt. This position was directly opposite the entrance to the Neville's Cross Workingmen's Club, which was accessed by travelling up a small number of steps. We always found this a good position on a Monday night because this was the night when the Club put on a live group to accompany the dancing and the function always attracted a good number of attractive girls who had to walk past the end of the wall, cross the road and up the steps to gain access to the function. We were still at a time when anyone going out for the night took pride in their appearance from top to tail. High heeled shoes, seamed stockings and the recently arrived mini skirt were all present to make the scene all the more enjoyable, not to mention the fantastic hairstyles varying from natural flowing locks to heavily lacquered beehive creations.

As the umpteenth pair of girls clicked their way past and the sound of a group playing Shadows music could be heard from the open windows, my attention was suddenly taken by a police car with sirens sounding and lights flashing. It negotiated the awesome Neville's Cross traffic lights complex and headed off westwards. I wondered if I would have time to finish my meal or would I miss the end of 'Foot

Tapper' my favourite Shadows tune, before we got a call probably from some careless motorist who had hit another car or even a lamp post. Normally, I would have jumped into an L/R and followed the police car, probably arriving on the scene and securing the recovery job before some other garage got involved. However, with the smell of passing perfume and my type of music, I wasn't about to move on the off-chance of a job. My curiosity started to go into a higher gear when several others quickly followed the first police car. The police cars became intermingled with a steady stream of ambulances and I started to wonder what it was all about. Other forms of activity that were obviously connected with the same incident replaced the initial rush of emergency vehicles. The fire support tender passed by, as did police supervisory vehicles and then it all went fairly quiet. It was interesting to note that none of the ambulances came back. I closed the workshop doors and travelled to the filling station to see if any news had filtered through.

It must have been at least an hour after I had seen the first police car that I answered the telephone to find I was speaking to the most senior traffic police officer in County Durham. Rather ironically it was the same officer who some years earlier had brought to a halt the handing out of cigarettes. He had decided to go to a call box near to this incident and make direct contact rather than pass the information second hand via headquarters. He explained that our new heavy recovery vehicle would be needed as soon as possible at a notorious hill called Crawleyside Bank which is just to the north of and leading into Stanhope, a sizeable Weardale community some 25 miles west of Durham. He gave a brief description of what had happened. A coach had overturned and he indicated what was required and suggested I get there as soon as possible. As I climbed aboard our new Scammel I was rather thankful that it was no longer the Diamond T. It immediately burst into life and I was on my way at a speed somewhere just short of 30 miles per hour. However, just as I was leaving the vehicle holding area opposite Dafty's shop, Sir who was on his way to play snooker confronted me. He'd spotted the Scammel going mobile. I briefly outlined the job and he decided, not on my recommendation, that he would give his game a miss and drive to the scene in his Jaguar to assist me with the recovery of the coach. He rode off toward Weardale without discussing anything further.

Despite the work being quite interesting and often relatively high profile I suppose I had settled into a routine where I was unmoved by whatever happened, yet on this occasion I felt like I was starting again. I was using a new state-of-the-art recovery vehicle and heading to a job that I didn't know what I was going to find. As I travelled the 20 miles, I noticed junctions lined with people who had come out to watch the comings and goings. As I got nearer the scene the activity became more intense. Unfortunately by the time I arrived it had changed from dusk to total darkness but it was still a warm and pleasant night.

When travelling from the north, Crawleyside Bank is arrived at after a long run over open moorland. Long before the bad part of the Bank is reached the road starts to fall away and it is easy to see how a vehicle can build its speed up. After the shallow deceptive descent the road goes slightly left and at the same time over a brow on to the first steep part of the hill. The Bedford coach was full of old age pensioners who lived in the seaside mining community of Blackhall, some 40 miles east of where the incident occurred. It subsequently transpired that they were a senior citizens' bowling team and had just enjoyed victory in an away match. What they were doing descending this piece of hill I could never quite understand. Subsequent investigations found that the driver once over the crest of the hill had attempted to reduce the speed of the coach, which was never suggested as being excessive, by changing down the gearbox and selecting a lower gear. However, this type of gearbox, which was universally used in all buses and commercial vehicles of its day, did not enjoy the synchromesh selection of later transmissions and required a very high input of driver skill. The procedure would have been to depress the clutch and move the gear stick to neutral. It would then be necessary to increase the engine speed to what would be expected of the new gear, quickly release the clutch and harmonise the speed of the various cogs, quickly re-depress the clutch and engage the new gear at a time when all cogs and mechanisms were rotating at a matching speed. The process is called double declutching and was the only method which allowed a down change at any sort of speed.

The process is fraught with problems and dangers. Firstly in order to bring the engine speed up, the right foot has to be taken from the brake and moved to the accelerator, during which time the vehicle is in neutral and would undoubtedly increase in speed. If the first attempt at aligning the cogs and gears fails, which in practice it often did (most people of that day will have heard a bus or lorry grinding its gears as the driver attempts to change speeds), the whole process has to be started again. Under normal circumstances this would not present any problem and a driver worth his salt would get a gear selected at no more than the third attempt, but in carrying out this manoeuvre, especially if the vehicle is going down hill, the brake pedal like the accelerator pedal has to be pressed once or twice. It is therefore very easy to starve the braking system of its air or vacuum support, which is probably what happened on this occasion.

While all this was happening it would be just a few seconds and the speed of the vehicle would have increased beyond the capacity of the gear that the driver was about to select. He would have no other option either to remain in neutral or put the vehicle back into the higher gear and then rely on the braking system, which on this occasion had probably already been exhausted. The coach had continued down the steep gradient probably not reducing speed by very much or even increasing its speed as it went. It must have been a frightening sight.

The steep part of the hill is followed by an awkwardly cambered 60 degree right hand corner, which is somewhat difficult to take at any time as it goes between the various houses on the left hand side of the road and some individual properties to the right. This ageing coach was made of wood and aluminium and coach built on to the manufacturer's chassis consisting of two beams running front to back with the engine and front axle at one end and the rear axle at the other end. The only other materials used were the glass of the windows and some steel holding the cushions up in the various seats. Since the driver was helpless to take the tight and difficult right hand corner, the vehicle must have started to disintegrate as soon as it made contact with the various structures on the left hand side of the road. A head-on impact with the houses was only avoided because of the various stone walls and other stone structures that form the entrances to the various properties which were still only a few feet back from the road.

I was approaching the scene from the Stanhope side and had to travel up the very steep gradient of the lower half of the bank to get to the scene. Everything had been completely floodlit, not just by the emergency services but also by television crews which had already arrived. I was surprised that they'd got there so quickly because some had travelled much further than I had but were obviously well installed. As I made my way along the last hundred yards on foot, I kept coming across radio and television personalities who, over the years, had been breakdown customers. Charlotte Allan was putting together some report for Tyne Tees Television. I saw Kate Adie, not because this was a war zone but because she was still a junior reporter on BBC Radio Durham. Even before I reached the heart of the incident I was already climbing over parts of the coach that had continued down the hill. Further up, the bulk of the coach had finished up in a ball, after going over the top of a garden wall, down into the garden some four feet below, and jamming itself against the main building.

I have never attended an aviation incident but it cannot be much different to this. The emergency services had stripped away as much of the wood and aluminium as they could in order to release the injured and trapped passengers. To make matters worse the coach was still almost upside down. As I scrambled around assessing the scene I noticed that the impact had been so high a large crack had developed in the house that had been hit. The Chief Superintendent who had earlier telephoned me brought me up to date on the casualty list. He believed there were probably up to two dozen people who had died and many more were seriously injured. He was anxious that there were no more people either trapped alive or dead under the remains of the coach. He needed the vehicle to be carefully lifted so that appropriate people could carry out a search. As I was about to reverse into the position where our new Scammel would be able to totally lift the remains from the house, Sir arrived on the scene, having been initially refused admission to the site. He had had to walk about a mile from the bottom of the hill. We immediately clashed over the procedure that should be used to recover the vehicle and subsequently the first attempt proved unsuccessful as the vehicle was solidly wedged between the house and the remains of the wall. The police didn't appreciate this failure. The half-hearted lift meant having to put the vehicle down again, which would not have suited anybody who was trapped underneath.

For the first time since being employed by this company harsh words were exchanged between my employer and me but we were under so much pressure to lift the thing back on to the road. We were using a vehicle that I was not fully familiar with, combined with working sideways on a very steep part of the hill, which is normally recognised as a recipe for disaster in the recovery industry at the best of times. We soon came to our senses and subsequently got the vehicle rolled out on to the road. Fortunately there were no bodies or people to deal with. I trawled the remains down the hill to where there was a wide grass verge and placed everything down. I then made several journeys because the vehicle, in one way or another, had finished up in separate pieces. During the next few hours everything would be placed on the grass verge for inspection or assessment. Nobody of course knew what had happened at this stage.

It was now half past two in the morning and there wasn't anything else that I could do, so I returned to the workshop where already curious people had gathered having seen reports of this incident on national television. Colin P., who was cursed with the most inquisitive nature, did not give me a break, when really at this stage I had only seen it as a difficult job that was now almost completed. After cranking up a well earned brew, the phone rang and I took a call, someone had run out of petrol some five miles away - another job that had to be done.

I then realised how tired and exhausted I had become with dashing up and down the hill and carrying seats and doors and bus parts, and I just crashed out in the canteen. The next thing I knew, it was half past seven and the Service Manager was banging on the workshop door to be let in. I knew that I would have to go back to the scene and continue salvage duties. This had been arranged for around 11 o'clock in the morning so after getting a further couple of hours sleep I set off back towards Stanhope.

On arriving, things were very different. The whole area had been sealed off and in any case people had already lost interest. The Department of Transport had arrived on the scene and one or two police officers were still in evidence. I hadn't had much time to consider it until now but I was informed that 18 elderly people had lost their lives and hardly anyone from the entire coach had escaped injury. Council workers were also present tidying the scene and brushing up debris. Everyone involved will, I suppose, have their own memories of what constituted the worst of the tragedy. It must have been grim for the first people there trying to get the passengers out of that tangle of aluminium. Thankfully it was part of the scene that I did not witness but as everything was tidied up and some of the people's belongings were put down at the side of the road to be sorted, I was taken back by the number of false teeth. There must have been at least ten sets. There were quite a number of pipes and other personal items that had not yet been identified and I suddenly felt that this was not just a job it was a terrible job. After seeing these items I was just rather pleased to get the whole thing finished with.

The rest of the day was spent loading mechanical parts on to a lorry to be taken away for investigation and then my final job was to take the non-mechanical parts straight to the scrap yard where they were immediately crushed. Apart from the large mechanical components like the engine and the gearbox, I remember the next biggest item being part of the roof and back part of the rear of the coach, everything else was just like matchwood. I have thought since that this must be what it looks like when an aircraft crashes.

I was too busy to read newspapers on the incident and we didn't have a television at work so I was not bombarded with news stories of the event, so in many ways once I was finished with the job, the situation just went away. I have to remind myself that despite the gravity of the situation and the involvement of the emergency services that were first on the scene, everybody just took the job in hand and got on with it. I don't remember anybody needing counselling. The only 'counselling' was the Council workers that came and swept the road.

The whole saga had a very unusual twist and I certainly remember that this story made the papers. Some two weeks later when a luxury coach was descending the hill into Stanhope on the south side, it suffered a momentary brake failure and the front wheels slid over what would be an almost sheer fifty foot drop but it stopped on the edge just like in the film 'The Italian Job' and all the passengers got out safe and sound. Once again a coach had to be recovered and once again it was all in a night's work, but this time it had a more pleasant ending.

# CHAPTER XII

Not that it had any place in history, but just after the coach accident things started to change considerably. The Durham Motorway, which was to run from Scotch Corner to Newcastle, was already half finished and in a couple of years' time would completely bypass Durham City. In the meantime, while various sections were under construction, traffic was diverted in all sorts of directions after using one or two of the newly opened sections at the south end. When anyone had a car failure or more usually an accident in the roadworks they had no idea where they were. So this often became very frustrating as we attempted to interrogate people. We would ask questions like, "Are you in the AA?" to which they would reply, "No, I'm in the Bay Horse." In these situations one frustration can lead to another. Another old chestnut that we always had to cope with was when someone had a punctured wheel. We would ask if they had a spare. They would usually reply, "Yes." So we would arrive on the scene prepared for a wheel change and would ask where the spare wheel was, only to be told, "That's the spare on the nearside front, the one with the puncture. The front wheel is at home because it also suffered a puncture six months ago and I forgot to repair it." The situation would then get worse because we had quoted a price for a wheel change, which was £1.12.6d. The vehicle now needed to be recovered, which could cost in excess of £2.10.0d. Sometimes it would be as much as three or four pounds and as usual, no money was forthcoming.

Not all my memories are so depressing. The night that Neil

Armstrong landed on the moon the whole world was waiting in anticipation of that first step. There was very little traffic on the roads as people huddled round black and white televisions waiting for the great event. I was lucky to be called to fit a fan belt to a Hillman Minx at a house that had such a television just inside a large bay window. As I beavered away loosening the dynamo and installing the new belt the owner was dashing in and out of the house giving me a running commentary. So just at the critical moment I was able to press my nose against the glass and see what was happening. I don't remember much of the picture because it was too blurred. I certainly did not hear any of the comments about "One small step for man and a giant step for mankind." but I do know where I was when it happened. Being interested in space travel and aircraft I turned my thoughts back to when the American astronaut Alan Shepard had gone into space while I was fitting a clutch. Once again history was being recorded and this time I was fitting a fan belt.

I suppose another land mark which I recall as one of the saddest days was when I heard that the Grand Prix racing driver Jim Clark had been killed while racing at Hockenheim in Germany. This time I was not even at work but taking part in an Autocross meeting. I was just about to start a race when the official that asks if you are ready to race once the lights change, informed me through the car window that Jim Clark was dead. Fortunately he also told the other four drivers and all of us had an equally poor run before the meeting was abandoned for the rest of the day.

I had now taken part in quite a few overnight rallies but the schedule was very demanding and I had decided that in order to fulfil my quest for a regular supply of motor sport activity I would change to a Mini

Cooper S which would be a car more than suitable for winning any Autotest Meeting that I took part in. It would also be suitable for competing in a small selection of national rallies, which are larger events held in different parts of the country. For the latter I could use up some annual holiday, after all I had a full two weeks available each year. I was lucky to be able to buy an accident-damaged Mini Cooper S that was written off by someone driving uninsured. His only option was to sell the remains to someone, if not me then somebody like me, who would then fit a new body shell and return the vehicle to the road. This is exactly what I managed to do, making the vehicle as identical as possible to the Minis that had been so successful in the Monte Carlo Rally just a few years previously.

I had limited success competing in the few national rallies, mainly because my vehicle was not in the high state of tune of other competitors and I still lacked experience of the British Forestry Commission roads, which were used for these events. However, as far as Autotesting was concerned, among many other things, I won a round of the British Autotest Championship and was selected to represent Britain who would be competing against Sweden. Unfortunately the event was to take place in Sweden and it would have taken too much time out of my impossibly tight schedule, so I had no option but to decline and let someone else have the place.

I have never had any regrets, in fact I have hardly ever given it another thought because one of the foremost things on my mind was to take part in the Lombard RAC Rally that I would be doing as a Privateer. Preparations for this event, which was to be run at the end of November, started as early as August. I had persuaded a local travel agent to provide sponsorship and I needed a team of four volunteers who would, using two of their own vehicles, meet me at various points around the route to provide spare parts and repairs as necessary. They were known as service crews and were just as excited and enthusiastic as my co-driver and me.

The driver of one of the service crews was to be Hovis who, apart from his personality and enthusiasm, was a useful assistant because of the welding and engineering skills acquired in the family business. He also drove a Vauxhall Viva Estate car that would be suitable for carrying welding gear and other components. We had agreed that we would fit Vauxhall Victor rear springs in order to be able to carry the welding bottles and spare suspension parts. We didn't really have a full range of spare parts so I decided that all components for the offside of the car would go in Hovis's Viva Estate and all components for the nearside would go in the other service vehicle, a Renault 16. which also had a good carrying capacity.

Over the coming weeks the Mini Cooper was stripped to the last nut and bolt then meticulously assembled to the highest standard that we could achieve, given my modest surroundings. The vehicle was then tested by driving up and down some of the roughest farm roads that I could find in the area. Following this we were confident that we would be able to cover the 600 plus miles on forestry maintenance roads and approximately 2,000 on public roads without too much difficulty.

The start of this event, which was the 1970 Rally, was from London Heathrow Airport from where we departed on the Saturday morning. Our first rest halt would be Perth in Scotland on the Sunday evening. My two service crews would be zigzagging around the route and would meet us after each of the special stages to check over the vehicle and add fuel. However, after leaving Heathrow Airport the first forestry stage was not until Clipstone Forest near Nottingham. We therefore expected a gentle Saturday drive, but my confidence turned to dismay when halfway to Nottingham the alternator stopped charging and we were forced to rendezvous and fit our only spare unit. So after covering only 100 miles we now had no spare alternator. I also noticed that while travelling at continually high speed on the motorway the engine oil pressure was not what it should be. I started to have visions of being back home by Saturday night and resigned to listening to the results on the radio.

I think from this point onwards my instincts as a motor mechanic started to take over instead of my desire to do well in rallying. I had consciously and sub-consciously decided that at all costs I must travel the complete route and finish the Rally. The first thing I did was to take a piece of tape and mark the rev-counter at 5,000 rpm. The engine normally performed to 6,000. I had reckoned that with a reduction of some 20% everything on the car would last so much longer and if I used the higher gears I should not lose too much time. I was amazed at how effective this was and by the time we arrived at Perth we needed hardly any maintenance, the car seemed to be improving and I was starting to pick up speed as I was getting used to the stages. I was further helped by several stages that were covered in sheet ice and snow. Apart from enjoying driving on this sort of surface it put little or no strain on the car. It even surprised us after starting at number 141 we had worked our way into the top 75.

The route continued on to the west of Scotland, by which time it was midnight on the Sunday and I'd had not a wink of sleep. Once we had stopped at Bathgate I became dead to the world, so much so that my co-driver had to drive the next road section, finally getting me woken up just a few minutes before the next special stage. We continued through the night and on to the marvellously scenic stages of the Lake District, by which time it was Monday afternoon. These stages were also covered in sheet ice, but this time I was absolutely terrified by the hundreds of feet drop from the ice-covered roads. It would be easy to make a mistake and finish up in one of the lakes some few seconds later.

The first full overnight halt was on the Monday night at Blackpool where the cars were impounded and placed on the Promenade for everyone to see but of course not touch. We had worked our way up to 63rd place and were something like 7th or 8th in Class. After we had cleaned a fish and chip shop out we all went off to bed feeling fairly pleased that we had got this far. Up to now most routes had been either frozen hard, ice-covered or had a covering of snow. This had meant that the strain on the car had been relatively light. As we got ourselves cranked up and under way at six the next morning, we were heading to North Wales and all of this was about to change. I was about to endure the worst two days of driving that I have ever experienced. We probably, up to now, had covered 350 miles so we still had another 250 left. The rally stages seemed to have an average range of about 10 to 15 miles and half way through the second of the day's stages, which were unbelievably rough as the temperature had risen and deep mud started to appear, there was a loud crack at the rear, followed by a series of banging. I realised that a suspension component had broken.

We continued at reduced speed and met our service crew. It was likely we would be able to change the damaged suspension component but some of the brake system had also disappeared, so we were reduced to three brakes, two at the front and one at the rear. We had not gone far into the next special stage when the alternator light reappeared but careful observation of the gauges and systems indicated to me that the fan belt had broken, of which we were carrying a spare. I simply pulled to the side of the road, jumped out and fitted the fan belt and off we went once again. For all that travelling with three brakes was not a big problem it became tiring because every time the brake pedal was pressed the car slewed to one side and it had to be corrected. As the day wore on I started to become physically tired with the very rough stages and the difficult handling of the car. But worse was to come.

With any rally car with three brakes or four the continuous working of the steering wheel would be nothing less than what would be expected but I suddenly started to feel a cracking sensation and realised that one of the three aluminium spokes on the steering wheel had fractured, leaving only two. At the end of the special stage a further examination revealed that a second spoke was about to fail which would leave only one. I managed using a pair of mole grips, which is the most universal tool any rally driver can ever carry, to secure the least damaged of the spokes. Then, taping the thing altogether, finished up with a usable steering wheel. In the meantime Hovis had given himself the task of finding a replacement from what appeared to be numerous scrap yards along the route. It was unlikely he would find a Mini Cooper S, so I gave him a list of vehicles that I believed would have a steering wheel that would fit the rally car.

I had no cause to complain when two stages later he met me with a steering wheel from a Morris 1000. I was rather relieved that the splines and fittings were the same but the wheel was about 2 feet in diameter and I had to be very careful not to jam my fingers on the windscreen or the side of the door. Once I got used to it, it was no problem at all and the larger diameter made the strain on my arms and shoulder much less. So all we had to do now was await the next problem, which was not too long in coming.

Just as darkness fell and we were right in the middle of a long and arduous stage, there was another bang, this time from the front and the car slumped down. I knew what had happened, one of the suspension units had failed but the service crew was carrying spares. We continued at reduced speed until we came out of the forest and rendezvoused with Hovis in his Viva Estate. We had worked out that in 6 or 8 minutes we would be away but as we removed the wheel and started to work on the suspension my feelings once again turned to despair. The suspension unit had failed and during our efforts to get out of the stage, the steel mounting had become damaged and mangled and we could not remove the damaged unit, it was going to be a few hours job. We then had to go back and do a further 40 miles before there was a 30-minute window where we would perhaps be able to do something. We scraped and scratched along, being overtaken by a car every eight or ten minutes, probably 15 cars in all, until we finally got clear and reached the service area.

As we started to ponder the situation we realised that the other side unit was also failing and we had an inkling that this also could not be changed. We knew we couldn't continue with the car scraping the ground for another 150 miles. I then decided that if the car could be lifted clear of the ground at least we might stand some chance of continuing until a solution could be found. We still had 20 minutes left. I decided that we would take a fencing post which had been preserved by creosoting and make two specially shaped wedges which would go between the top suspension arm and the vehicle sub frame and would raise the vehicle to its maximum height, giving us four or five inches of ground clearance but of course no suspension travel. We secured the wooden chocks in place in such a way they could not become detached and we felt quite pleased with ourselves. The rear of the vehicle was still a tad on the low side so we had to bend the spot lights down, otherwise they were only lighting up the treetops. There was a further 50 miles to the next series of stages and I was quite amazed at how well the vehicle travelled on the road. It was much better than it had ever been, though I did notice that it didn't like potholes or manholes. We talked about the situation and believed that we had overcome the problem. But as I left the start of the first special stage once again I realised what a bad assumption we had made. While the vehicle had been great on the smooth highways it was almost impossible to cope with on the bumpy special stages. Every single bump was magnified and went right through not just the vehicle but through the bodies of the crew.

When there was a piece of road that was smooth and straight it would usually catch us out because while a healthy car might have jumped six inches in the air, we jumped three feet, and when we landed we jumped another two and then another one until we finally settled. But we were still running and out of the 218 cars that started the Rally there were now less than 80 so we felt we had to try and keep going. After a while, even though we had resigned ourselves to our lack of speed, we didn't get overtaken by many cars as other competitors were also starting to hit problems.

The physical strain was tremendous and after covering 80 or 90 miles I lost concentration and finished up going off backwards dropping probably 20 feet into some bushes. As we came to rest with the vehicle on its side we thought "That was it." However, there were at least 500 people on the corner and just a few yards from us were two other cars, which had crashed heavily, so we were not alone. While my mechanical skills had seen us get this far it was my recovery training that was about to save us this time. I had always carried a long rope and the one we had on this occasion was something like 25 yards. I always believed that a long rope some day would be useful so all I had to do was to tie one end of the rope on one rear wheel, one end on the other rear wheel and then I threaded it round 30 or so willing volunteers who just walked off like a pack of workhorses and pulled the Mini back up the hill and onto the road, bramble bushes and all. It probably took us longer to unhook the rope and fold it back up than it took us to get the car out. I remember we lost no more than six or seven minutes which was considerably less than we lost when the suspension failed in the first place. So once again we were on our way. Many years later when I was speaking at a Motor Club Dinner I was approached by a middle-aged man who claimed that as a youth his father had been one of the 30 people pulling on the rope and had recounted the story many times how he had never come across any other competitor who was carrying a decent sized rope.

The nights are always long on an RAC Rally. It was held at the end of November when daylight disappeared not long after four in the afternoon and didn't reappear again until nine the next day. This night seemed even longer. With our reduced speed and various problems we were beginning to fall to the back of the field but we still kept coming across other competitors who had failed completely. Despite the high physical input required we were somehow managing to keep going. I therefore could not believe that as we took a medium soft left hand corner a front steering arm snapped and we once again veered off the road but this time onto a piece of rough shale. I was sure now that our rally was over but as I emerged from the car we encountered the most unbelievable piece of luck. We were in the middle of a 30 mile long special stage and we had failed some 50 yards from where the forest came near the public road. As I looked down the hillside I could see service crews working on the main road. I knew if I scrambled to the road our service crew might not be too far away. What I didn't expect was to climb the fence on to the road and find Hovis and his co-driver asleep waiting for me to arrive some 30 minutes later as I would have done had I completed the correct route.

Once I had woken them up and explained our dilemma we were even more fortunate to find it was Hovis's side of the car that had failed. We all scrambled back into the stage with toolboxes and parts and had a new hub assembly fitted. The car was underway again even though we had no time to reset the tracking. We were toeing out by about half an inch, but this was just a matter of the crew waiting for me to complete the full route. The car would then be serviced at the correct place. Though we couldn't imagine it at the time, this was to be our last major disaster. By the time we arrived at the motorway services near the Severn Road Bridge it was Wednesday morning and we had had little more than 8 hours sleep since starting on the Saturday. We still had some 30 stage miles to cover and I was virtually living on Mars Bars and orange juice which, rightly or wrongly, I believed contained all the necessary ingredients to go on forever. I suppose we counted down those 30 stage miles the way a prisoner would count his 30 years in prison. I can even remember the last special stage having only five miles left and I kept asking my co-driver on numerous occasions, "How much further, how much further?" We did eventually get back to Heathrow but by the time we arrived, and we were still on time and classified, some competitors had been back for hours. We eventually finished just inside the top 50 but that didn't matter, the main thing was we had actually finished when 60% of the entry hadn't made it. We were the only crew from the North East to complete the RAC Rally that particular year. We were the talk of Durham on our return but never, ever would I want to go through that again. Subsequently I took part in a further ten RAC Rallies and managed to complete nine but all the rest together were not as hard as the first one.

Despite the pounding we had suffered on the 1970 RAC Rally I couldn't wait to place an entry when the entry forms and regulations came through the post for the 1971 event. Spurred on by my previous year's achievement, the Durham Motor Club had five crews who were all entering, so getting helpers in the form of service crews was at a premium. Once again I managed to put an enthusiastic team together, though Hovis finished up with a navigator assistant whose enthusiasm rather exceeded his ability, but we all bonded as a team and we had the advantage over other Club members of having one year's experience of the event. Even though nothing was kept secret in the way of preparation, they didn't take it as seriously as we did because they just didn't realise how arduous and difficult the RAC Rally would be. Using this experience and my mechanical skills we built the car to a much tougher specification. We also incorporated the ability to change difficult parts much easier and as we were still using the same Mini Cooper S, at least we understood everything about the car.

The one big advantage was that the rally would start and finish at

Harrogate, which was only 60 miles away. As the Saturday of the start was upon us I could not believe my luck, it started to snow rather heavily and seemed to continue all day as we ran through the stages in North Yorkshire. By 8 o'clock at night there was at least 12 inches of snow everywhere and it had drifted in several places. Cars were having difficulty just getting up some of the hills and I started to learn about the value of having the correct tyres. We had elected to use some remould tyres because of the cost saving and we found the cheaper, softer, poorer quality rubber was just what was needed to cover ice and snow stages quickly. It just seemed that other people were either too frightened to drive quickly and/or had tyres that were totally unsuitable. We would leave the start of special stages and after two or three corners would come across a struggling competitor. I was not amused that some of the stages were deemed impossible and were cancelled. At one point so many cars were struggling in the Yorkshire forests that we were given an official instruction to miss some stages and drive to the checkpoints at Scotch Corner. We were almost the first car there which was tremendous for morale because the less educated thought we were well inside the top ten, whereas we were simply running with the top ten cars on the road.

We left Scotch Corner to drive through the notorious Keilder stages and the various stages in the south of Scotland, which were all covered in deep snow. We arrived late morning in the city of Perth where there was a distinct absence of other competitors. However, because the timing on the road sections had been readjusted they would eventually catch up and re-establish themselves in the correct running order. As we arrived for the Sunday night supper halt at Grantown-on-Spey, with the temperature well below freezing, we were amazed to find that we had achieved 21st overall out of about 200 cars that had started. Most of these cars were still running as we arrived at the checkpoint. Much to my dismay, because of the ever-deteriorating weather, many of the following night's stages were cancelled. We finished up back at Blackpool for the Monday night halfway halt inside the top 30, having had a very trying day on the ice-covered Lakeland stages, many of which featured sheer drops down to the freezing water. As in the previous year when we restarted the Welsh loop, the snow had disappeared and we were back to the hard damaging special stages. This year driver and car were ready, much better prepared, mentally, physically and mechanically. The only thing that happened was that we were left trailing for speed as the more powerful cars started to find their feet now the ice had gone.

We eventually arrived back at Harrogate on the Wednesday afternoon nowhere near as tired and exhausted as the previous year. However, we had dropped down to just inside the top 50 but once again we had completed the rally and again were the only Durham crew to do so. I had driven the entire rally without once putting a wheel off the road, even if at times that was at the expense of a bit of extra speed. Our only casualty had been Hovis when his mechanic-cum-navigator had started to get exhausted as the alcohol had drained slowly from his blood stream. He had made an error in plotting a six-figure reference that was scheduled to be the rendezvous point and his mistake was so bad that his projected rendezvous point was some 60 miles in the opposite direction to where it should be. By chance, it was on a road adjoining a forest so they settled down for the night on the assumption that we would waken them up when we arrived or at least the noise of other competitors and activity would normally wake them. Instead, they were not woken until a farmer driving his cows towards being milked caught the side of the Viva with his stick. Hovis's first assumption was that the rally had passed and we had had no problem. So further time was lost before they realised exactly where they were at, which was now some 180 miles from where they should have been at this time. With no mobile communication of any sort we just had to continue with one service crew until Hovis and his red faced assistant turned up some 14 hours late.

Using the same car, at least the same body shell, we again entered the Rally in 1972. Proving that experience and practice can make perfect we completed the whole rally and hardly put a spanner on the vehicle. Because there was no snow, no ice, just rain, we were left struggling for pace and finished outside the top 50 but managed 3rd in Class. This was mainly due to people moving away from the smaller classes as the Ford Escort started to become dominant. Once again we had completed the rally; in fact we completed the three rallies using the same car. However I decided that I would never ever take part in a forest rally again using a Mini of any sort. So, shortly after the event, I advertised and sold the car complete with its numbers, scrapes and dirt. An era had ended.

# CHAPTER XIII

By now I had been doing this breakdown job for some six years and apart from the replacing of the Diamond T nothing much had changed. But as the company was now expanding from its original 20 staff to well over 60, with three or four different depots, all sorts of moves were afoot. Sir had decided that we needed to move to a purpose-built breakdown centre which he had earmarked in one of his other buildings just opposite Dafty's shop, where the breakdown vehicles were often parked. He felt that with the approaching of the motorway we would need to have a fully professional image. So a selection of breakdown controllers to man the telephone and the radio would be employed. I would have to move from my beloved canteen where I'd got quite used to getting a good night's sleep even if it was broken in three parts. I suppose that at face value it seemed to be the way to go, but I'd not allowed for a daytime controller who was short of a full loaf and a night-time controller who was a compulsive alcoholic. Albert had long since left the company and a series of opposite numbers had been employed, with little success.

To make matters worse, Sir had decided that I should now be in charge of this operation. This was a thankless task because of my inexperience in management and the sub-standard temperament of the people that I was supposed to be in control of. Perhaps the most difficult person I had to deal with was the night-time controller who was referred to as 'Walls'. An ex-miner, he was a typical North East old-fashioned Labour councillor. Somehow he'd been elected by the local community from an old pit village where the only pastime of any worth was owning greyhounds or pigeons, or both and being a regular and conscientious Working Men's Club member.

Walls would work five nights beginning like other breakdown staff at five o'clock and finishing at eight the next morning. Like the breakdown staff he was allowed to rest after midnight. Sir had done a deal whereby his pay was reduced to half at midnight and returned to its normal rate at seven in the morning, inferring that he should be up and about before the shifts changed. He would always arrive carrying what I assumed was his 'bait' in a regular khaki bag with a shoulder strap. He indicated that it was his supper. True, it was his supper and when I came to move the bag I found it contained two bottles of Newcastle Brown Ale, the standard beverage of a heavy drinking North East man.

If Walls was feeling a little peckish towards the end of the first part of the evening he would pop into the local pub, which unfortunately was in the adjoining building, to pick up a pie. He would, by chance, finish up with two or three bottles of ale just to help the pie down. This would be on top of the regular two bottles that he brought to work. So by half past eleven he was not fit to talk to never mind answer the phone. I made various efforts to draw this to the attention of Sir but he was so busy running his empire that he could not be bothered as long as the job was getting done. Walls's rate of pay was something like a shilling an hour after midnight so he was cheap to run. Some of the breakdown staff, and by this time we had several, would spend time with him and be humoured by him but, quite frankly, I couldn't get far enough away. I would go over to the filling station or try to occupy myself polishing the trucks.

I'd found a suitable corner of the new building where I could put a bunk, which gave me an added excuse to get out of the road. The facilities, in keeping with the Company tradition, were on the sparse side. There was a small, old-fashioned toilet bowl and washbasin from which Walls persistently stated that he would pick up some disease. So he chose to operate in the toilet by standing on the seat, which consisted of two wooden slats, bolted to the sides of the bowl and which were always rather slippery for that particular style of relieving yourself. We all knew it was only a matter of time, given his inebriated state, before he lost his balance and slipped. But I ask the question, why did it have to be on my shift? And why did it have to be at three o'clock in the morning? I was awoken by yelling and shouting and allegations of; "I will sue anybody who comes near me." to find that he was lying half down the side of the bowl and trying, by pulling on the taps of the basin, to get himself restored to an upright position with some of his clothes down and some up.

Since Walls was over 60 years of age I should have had some sympathy and helped him to get up. But I got in the truck and went over to the filling station where I stayed for the rest of the night until he had cleaned himself up and got himself off home at 8 o'clock. I never discussed the matter with him but I made certain that everyone else knew what had happened. During this whole period I can only assume that it was the outstanding reputation of the Company that avoided the business closing down. How it must have sounded for a motorist to call an established breakdown service and have a drunken man answer the phone beggars belief. They must have been very relieved when a 'proper person' turned up and they were remobilised and on their way with no fuss or bother.

With hindsight I suppose it was about this time that I started to question whether I was still enjoying the job. The conflict with Walls was un-resolvable and while I had no formal title I was expected to coordinate the running of the breakdown service in a smooth and efficient manner. Walls obviously had a dislike for everything I stood for and had an overwhelming desire to see Wislon drop dead. I had always admired Wislon for his ability to see a situation clearly but I never understood why he had to reinforce his point of view, which incidentally was right and correct, on somebody who was too thick even to understand what he was talking about. Wislon wouldn't tolerate anything said by Walls that he did not like or agree with. Nor would he let it lie at any price. When this happened Walls would merely add a couple of extra bottles of brown ale to his diet until he was too drunk to disagree.

Another cause of conflict with Walls, but of course with nobody else, was that I had given Wislon the job of overnight controlling on the two weekend nights when Walls was off. It was like a breath of fresh air to everybody to have a proper controller. When Wislon was unavailable we employed a student called Sam who did the occasional night or two.

The move to these revised premises, apart from having to endure Walls, generally enhanced the image of the operation. For the first time we had a direct line telephone number for the sole purpose of emergency breakdown calls. Though the premises were old, extremely old, they were just the right size for working on a couple of broken down cars. However, one area that took a down turn was my overnight resting accommodation. I had, over a six-year period, carefully refined my old mini rear seats, replacing them from time to time with later models that featured more padding and insulation and were an altogether up-market 'kipping' area. The only place I could find after the move to the revised site was a rather large cupboard area like a small store room that had no windows and was used for harbouring old car parts. Together with Gregory, my opposite number at the time, we set about trying to tidy the place out and manufacture a purpose-made bunk, which was the right size to take what we loosely termed as the original mattress *a la* Mini seat squabs. In some way we made it a home-from-home, putting in a reading lamp and a few coat hooks so it was an ideal place to get away from Walls.

Over the next few weeks I'd noticed that my socks were continually finishing up full of holes: one pair after another just never seemed to last five minutes. The cause of this puzzled me and it was only when I came across a former member of staff who had worked in the building that I discovered what was happening. It was when he informed me that I was sleeping in what used to be the car battery store-room that I realised I was jumping out of bed and standing on a floor that over 50 years had become impregnated with battery acid. While the remaining acid was not strong enough to cause any form of discomfort, it contained enough venom to take the goodness out of any cloth or material that was left near it for any length of time. So, in essence, the acid was being transferred into my leather boots and then being transferred back to socks that I was wearing on day shift. Over a six-month period I'd written off about a dozen pairs. Once we knew the problem it was easily resolved with a double layer of fitted carpet taken from the first vehicle that became a casualty with such sought after stock on board.

With the added stress of trying to maintain some semblance of order my main confidant and the person I would bounce ideas off was of course Wislon. Even though he had no motor trade background, he was a very intelligent man and worldly wise. As soon as he turned up at his usual time Walls would disappear into the pub which, as far as I was concerned, was the best option. However, when a job was taken I had to go and get Walls back out of the pub and he would return to the phone carrying the remains of his pint and would take another snipe at Wislon as he passed. I was never sure how the situation was going to pan out but it appeared to most people that it was going to end in some unpleasant manner with probably Walls in hospital and the rest of us getting the sack. Many scenarios were put forward, one of which included Walls tripping between the pub and the office, killing himself in the process, but we were not to be that lucky. Then fate took a most unusual twist that none of us had considered.

Like the Stanhope coach accident the memories of the next incident are just as well etched on my mind. Again, it was a mild summer night and I had just returned from a job involving the use of the heavy recovery vehicle. Walls had politely asked if it would be all right for him to go into the pub and buy a pie. I suggested that he take some extra money and pass me one out as his pie would probably take all night to eat and would be washed down with alcohol, whereas mine would be consumed alongside a pot of tea. I was munching away and watching the phone when a sudden cloudburst flooded the road outside the control room. It only lasted five or ten minutes but the rain really came down. When the phone next rang it was the police to say that a Mini 850 had left the road between Chester-le-Street and Durham. They were busy cutting the driver free and could I attend in about 30 minutes. This fitted nicely into the timetable as Wislon was due back shortly from a Council meeting and he would be a useful assistant to recover a car with this type of damage.

However, as the time passed I had to recover Walls from his watering hole and set off hoping Wislon would not turn up and get into a conflict. As I approached the scene there was considerable activity. There were so many police cars and emergency vehicles that I had to park and walk between them. It was only then that the unbelievable struck me. The duck egg blue Mini with the snow white roof was Wislon's vehicle. It was Wislon who had been involved in this serious accident and had been cut free and taken to hospital. He'd lost control in the flash flood and unable to correct a slide had slithered down the grass embankment, becoming impaled on a 2-inch diameter metal pole, which was part of the fencing lining the side of the road. The construction of the fence was quite simple. A concrete post every 12 or 15 feet and three horizontal metal pipes. One of these pipes had been damaged in a previous collision and was sticking out and Wislon had scored a bulls-eye on it. It made a neat hole in the driver's side door and a not-so-neat hole in the top half of his leg. It had passed completely through his right femur, fortunately somehow missing the left one, before continuing through the passenger side window.

Over the years I had dealt with many accidents, many much more serious than this and many involving fatalities. On numerous occasions I knew the people involved but never before had it been my best friend. Initially, after establishing the background, I got on and moved the vehicle and brought it back to the workshop and while it was still attached to the truck I went in to report the situation.

Fortunately John the storekeeper and Gregory the breakdown mechanic had called in. Also present was long-suffering GN who, of course, lived just across the road. They immediately recognised

Wislon's car and were concerned. Walls, however, already five or six pints the worse for wear, produced the most outstanding smile, in fact I think it was the only time I ever saw him smile, and offered to get in a round of drinks. At which point all hell broke loose and Walls was lucky not to be felled with a tyre lever as the shock of Wislon's situation started to grasp me. Only the presence of the other three people prevented another hospital case. GN made me aware that we didn't want Walls in the next bed to Wislon. I decided to unhook his vehicle and go to the hospital. GN decided he would come with me.

GN had called in after having a rather stressful day welding the inside of a steam boiler. He certainly looked as if he had been in a steam boiler. My appearance wasn't much better, as my boiler suit had developed a shine due to an overloading of oil and grease. We were both wearing strong leather boots in which new segs had been inserted. Segs are small spiked aluminium plates that are knocked into the soles of work boots to help them last longer and provide surer footing in slippery conditions. The ones in our boots were a gift from a grateful customer. As we arrived at the accident hospital, which was only half a mile from our depot, we found that we were rather unsuitably dressed and equipped to even be in a hospital. The floors were hard and tiled and the hobnailed boots with extra segs were worse than walking on ice and made enough noise to wake the whole place up. Fortunately it was still only about half past eight.

After various interactions we managed to make contact with Wislon who was lying sedated on a trolley in a corridor near the theatre. He was obviously in need of some type of operation to get him sorted out. I was then somewhat surprised to be called into an office and told that even though I was unrelated I would have to be considered his immediate next-of-kin. He needed urgent anaesthetic and I would have to sign to authorise the process. To this day I still find this rather odd. If I hadn't signed, would they not have carried out the operation? I did sign immediately but then, as we left, GN came up with numerous valid points. Once I had signed they would obviously go ahead but I wasn't his mother, what if he was allergic to the process? What if he was diabetic? What if he was of a religious disposition that didn't allow this sort of thing? GN, being a bit of a worrier, started to tell me that I would get slated if I had to attend an inquest relating to Wislon's death because I had signed the form. Would his parents sue me for signing on their behalf without their permission? I suppose in reality if I hadn't signed they would still have sorted him out. But the whole episode didn't make a lot of sense then and still doesn't make sense now.

So serious was the injury to Wislon that he was to remain in hospital for 16 weeks, where I visited him regularly. To save him money, I enlisted the help of a couple of girls from the motor club and moved him out of his extortionate bedsit establishment. His worldly goods were put in the back of my Mini Cooper S so that I could store them at my house. When he was eventually discharged from hospital we were pleased that he was able to stay with us until he got pulled round a tad, but he never again rode around with me in breakdown trucks. He returned to his job as a part-time controller but his career as a journalist was starting to take off. Eventually he found it necessary to make a career move to Dunfermline in Scotland on what was to be the second rung of a very successful journalistic career.

Two other odd memories remain which encompass this incident. Only a few days before Wislon left the road we were accosted by a salesman selling accident insurance. It was not very expensive, about five pounds for six months I recall and appeared to make a substantial payment if you were involved in any sort of accident. One particular clause gave a large sum of money if various criteria were met and the policyholder finished up in hospital. With me being involved in Motor Sport and Wislon riding about with me we decided insurance was a good idea. After paying the man and getting the policy, Wislon studied the small print. It clearly stated that to qualify for the large amount of benefit the accident had to occur while driving to and from work. The policy holder had to be the driver of the motor vehicle and not a passenger, it had to be between 8 in the morning and 8 at night and the injury had to be to one of about 10 listed parts of the body. To get the maximum benefit the claimant had to be in hospital for more than 21 days. Ironically Wislon met the criteria perfectly and since the policy was genuine, if somewhat ambiguous, an appropriate pay out was met without question. This would probably be one of only a few claims they were likely to get that would meet the criteria in such a perfect way.

In anticipation of these funds arriving Wislon asked if I could organise repairs to his motor vehicle. These were completed at a cost of 10 shillings for a new driver's door and two shillings and sixpence for a passenger side window, and his vehicle was as good as new, though of course it was nearly a year before he could drive it again.

# CHAPTER XIV

By 1970, almost ten years after the first stretch at Scotch Corner was opened, the A1(M) Durham motorway was fully completed in its entire length. The final two sections past Durham City to the east were finally opened giving a completed distance from top to tail of over 35 miles. This was 35 miles that could easily be covered in less than 35 minutes without once touching the brake or clutch pedal. This compared to the previous A1 road, which had numerous roundabouts, several sets of traffic lights and a good quantity of up and down gradients. All this was not without a few accident black spots and by and large it was this old A1 road that had been the backbone of the recovery business that I was working in. The night following the opening the whole area was like a morgue. The locals even seemed to have given the filling station a miss. There were no fish and bone wagons, no beer lorry, in fact no overnight lorries at all as they slipped effortlessly along this new stretch of motorway.

The magnitude of the change still comes back to me some 30 or more years later. While the old A1 road was constantly congested, once the traffic had been released to the motorway, even at lunchtime on a Friday, it was possible to stop on the hard shoulder, look in both directions, not see a single vehicle and execute an illegal U-turn.

With this complete change of circumstances we no longer had an abundance of work; in fact we hardly had any, though of course vehicles still did have some problems on surrounding side roads. In anticipation that in years to come business and activity would be built along the edges and junctions of the new motorway, Sir had purchased a few acres of land a few hundred yards from what in later years would be known as Junction 62. At the time of purchase this had been some sort of functioning garage but appeared originally to have been farm buildings. We decided that since the site was unoccupied, apart from a small showroom, it would be wise to move the breakdown operation to this new site. I was therefore faced with a second move in as many years.

On a personal note, I felt somehow that it was already the beginning of the end. The Company was getting larger by the day. It now employed over a hundred people at various sites across the county and whereas some years ago I had almost single-handed kept the body shop fully employed, I was now becoming insignificant. I was finding it difficult to work with some of the people that were employed and Walls was still with the Company. We were moved, lock, stock and all, to a semi-derelict shed on the new site. Because it was not wind and water tight we were given literally a garden shed measuring some 8ft by 6ft and about 6ft high where Walls could sit and answer the phone. There was just enough room in this garden shed for one other person to sit beside Walls, if that was what they so chose.

I therefore had a nightmare of a problem finding somewhere I could get my head down on the long night-shift. With Gregory's help I eventually constructed another shed in the opposite corner of this big building but the whole job was extremely primitive and as we were approaching winter it was always bitter cold. The only good thing was that we had all of the vehicles at the same site and of course we were close to the motorway. For the first time ever, if we recovered a broken-down articulated wagon, we could bring it back to our own site. To this end two commercial breakdown mechanics were employed to repair the trucks that we towed in. The business had moved from being mainly car-orientated to being mainly commercial vehicles.

As this was going on a large modern state-of-the-art workshop and body shop facility was being constructed on site, so for almost a year we were running the breakdown service from a building site. Several times Walls's garden shed had to be picked up and moved to a new location and my sleeping arrangements were also moved. I came to work one night and found my bunk in the skip and several hundred breeze blocks in its place, which didn't go down well at all. Morale was particularly low among all of the breakdown staff and the only person who benefited from the move was our old friend, Walls, who only had a mile to travel to work and was still right opposite a pub. Eventually a small car workshop was established beside the commercial unit and the new development started to take shape.

The full opening of the motorway changed the shape and type of work that I was now doing. For all we still recovered and dealt with cars, most of our energy was taken up with trucks. Many trucks now chose to use the motorway because of the quality of carriageway between London and Newcastle. We started to experience incidents that we had no previous experience of. The first incident happened when extremely high winds battered the region. These gales struck soon after the new carriageway had been opened. Some of the motorway contained elevated sections and as soon as a high-sided lorry entered this piece of road and was struck by a gust of wind it found itself lying on its side either on the hard shoulder in one direction or the central reservation in the other. Since these vehicles only overturned when they were empty they were very easy to restore to upright. I recall doing over a dozen in one afternoon. On some occasions, once upright, they would simply blow over again. The bigger articulated vehicles presented more of a challenge but were certainly a good source of revenue for our struggling operation.

The motorway certainly changed the way that we handled some of the jobs. There were many occasions when we could simply attach a rigid tow bar and tow the stricken vehicle on to its destination, largely travelling on wide flat roads. Sir called me into his office and suggested that we should source a vehicle, which could simply tow another vehicle along with no intention of lifting or winching. This necessitated another day out in the Right Honourable's new SJ6. Travelling as far as Bedford we visited the same manufacturer who'd produced our current Scammell. As a seasoned customer we were well received and an even larger Scammell was fully demonstrated, including multi-stage automatic transmission and an even stronger winch rope. It was indeed well equipped and had many features that our existing Scammell lacked. However, the asking price brought a sudden frown to our leader's forehead; he suggested it was time to go. Then, before I knew it, we were heading back up the A1.

However, as we were stuck in traffic near to Colsterworth, near Peterborough, we noticed a small Scammell tractor, the type that is often used by fairground people, sitting on a garage forecourt with a 'For Sale' notice attached. This was the type of tractor unit that is often connected at the rear of an abnormal load to help it up the hills and probably provided braking on the downhill. The vehicle was like a miniature of our existing Scammell. We swung into the forecourt, sat in the car, and talked about the endless possibilities of this vehicle. The big attraction was that it was priced around £600. This was about a tenth of the price of the vehicle we had assessed earlier that afternoon.

But would a £600 vehicle be any use? We thought not and continued on to Durham, stopping at a high-class fish restaurant that Sir had obviously acquainted himself with on more than one occasion. This time, once again not to waste a day, he educated me in the art of eating a fish without getting a mouthful of bones. It was amazing how in a few simple strokes of knife, fork and fingers, he filleted the lemon sole clear of every bone and then tucked in to enjoy the feast. He then noticed the problem I was encountering and offered me full guidance to repeat what he'd just done. I managed to rid the fish of about 60% of its bones, which was not bad for starters.

The next day he called me into his office claiming he'd had a bad night's sleep trying to work out whether the £600 would be well spent and we decided it would be a good investment, or at least a good risk. He had already noted down the telephone number and after a couple of phone calls he suggested that I find a friend to run me down to Colsterworth and he would give me some petrol money. I would need to do this on my day off, which was a Wednesday; otherwise it would interfere with the shift pattern. We duly arrived, handed over the cheque and set off back the 180 miles to Durham. Apart from being extremely noisy, the unit reached a speed of just over 30 miles per hour, which meant that it was going to be little more than a six-hour journey. While 32 miles an hour was fine for this Scammell it didn't suit Dave Bone who had gone with me. So he decided to make haste back home and leave me to chug along.

Even in the 1960s the A1 road had many miles of straight dual carriageway. It was after one of these long sections that I found something amiss with the steering and I only just managed to get through a roundabout. On getting out and checking the underneath I found that the nearside track rod nut had fallen off and the track rod was trailing on the ground. I was only steering on the offside wheel and the nearside wheel was finding its own direction courtesy of its geometry, which was fine until cornering was required. It had obviously been trailing for so long that the socket and a bit of the pole was almost worn away, but fortunately the thread and some of the pole was still present. There was no chance of getting a nut so I pushed it back into the steering arm and managed to find some twine from the fence at the side of the road. I wrapped and knotted it several times over and sure enough it lasted the 120 miles back to Durham. The 'repair' was so good it even travelled from one depot to another in Durham until we could get some new parts fitted.

Over the following years the vehicle became invaluable. We used to call it the 'chore horse' because it would do anything and it was so small and nimble. But it still had this ridiculous Scammell gear change, which featured a gating with an operating sequence similar to a maze where you went from one gear to another. This could only be done in the direction intended by the original designer. If the vehicle was stopped in sixth gear, every other gear from six downwards had to be selected from the sequence before first gear could be found. The maze-like gate was paramount in any gear selection. I was told a story of a Scammell driver who was sacked and his revenge was to park his truck on the side of the road and break the cast iron gate with a hammer, leaving the vehicle impossible to drive by even the most experienced operator. The story reads that the vehicle remained stuck on the roadside until a new gate could be obtained and fitted some three days later.

A more difficult recovery that came into the frame was when a vehicle for one reason or another would leave the carriageway and disappear down the embankment, often overturning in the process. If these incidents occurred at night they were usually left until daylight when the police could control the sparse but fast moving motorway traffic. One such box van had been discovered overturned at the bottom of a steep piece of embankment at three in the morning completely unattended. The police had tried to contact the Company without success but since it was Saturday night they had received no reply and we had no idea where the driver was. It was of some concern when we eventually corrected the vehicle the following afternoon to find out that somehow the driver had got from his cab and had fallen under the vehicle where he had become a fatality. We think the vehicle may have originally been upright but then toppled over as he was examining it.

While the new motorway was considered to be one of the safest pieces of road to travel on and I suppose pro rata to car numbers it still is, we started to notice that when an accident occurred it was often more severe. We never had a lorry overturn at 60 miles an hour on a roundabout and of course the motorway was equipped with a safety hard shoulder, which was perceived at the time to be a safe refuge in the event of a car having a problem. It was not long before we realised that because a car on the hard shoulder was stationery and the traffic flowed past at unabated speed some three feet away, it was not a place to stand for long. The ease of a fatality occurring came home to me when I stopped at an existing accident, which had already occurred on the hard shoulder when an Austin 1800 had found its way into the rear of a Bedford van. Fortunately I had driven past and stopped down the road from the incident and was walking back as the emergency services were trying to free the driver who was trapped by his feet in the pedals.

This accident had occurred when a healthy vehicle driven by an inattentive driver had already hit one broken down vehicle. Surely this wouldn't happen again and not at the same spot, but suddenly there was a squeal and another vehicle was coming down the hard shoulder towards us. To make matters worse the fuel pump that was under the rear of the 1800 had become dislodged and petrol was running back down the hard shoulder. As we lunged to get out of the way the third vehicle ploughed into the two vehicles, which were already on the hard shoulder and the whole lot started to burn. Within a matter of seconds the flames were so fierce that we couldn't get near to help the driver who was still completely trapped by his feet. It was only a matter of seconds before everything was a furnace and the slightly injured driver was gone. By the time the Fire Brigade arrived the vehicles had just about burnt out and we were all quite stunned to find what had happened. This incident occurred at about four in the afternoon. I was therefore surprised to find at the Coroner's inquest that the driver of the Austin 1800 was many times over the drink/drive limit despite the fact that he was a respected local councillor. It was a good lesson learned, not to trust a motorway hard shoulder as being a safe place. Even to this day when I see somebody sitting in a broken down car, my thoughts go back to what could so easily happen and sadly often still does.

Another source of income occurred when the motorway experienced its first sharp frost. The local Council had not yet perfected the art of salting and gritting in advance of ice forming, they would only turn out once sheet ice was firmly established. Since the motorway surface was new, smooth and flat, once a vehicle lost control it would travel hundreds of yards before it either slithered off the motorway, gyrated about its centre or, on some occasions, continued as if nothing had happened, though of course now at a snail's pace with an ashen faced driver at the wheel. Although I never experienced a multiple accident it was not unusual to see numerous vehicles spread about, each having had their own individual unrelated incident. We continued to get a selection of loaded vehicles falling foul of the conditions and from time to time managed to keep ourselves well stocked.

Even though Wislon was fairly well recovered from his incident, he rarely found any attraction in visiting me as he had done for so many years; he would still help to control on odd nights and now and again he would ride around with me. One of the last jobs I recall him assisting with was a Mercedes estate car belonging to a German tourist that had stopped on the hard shoulder just north of Scotch Corner. We had very little experience of any foreign car and certainly carried no spare parts. When the vehicle couldn't be fixed at the roadside a towrope was attached and Wislon jumped into the driving seat of the left-hand drive vehicle. We then travelled the 25 or so miles to Junction 62. Once up the slip road I set off to go round the interchange when I felt a tug and saw Wislon halfway up the embankment with the Mercedes. Fortunately no damage had resulted. Wislon, like all of us, had started to develop a short fuse. He jumped out complaining that I hadn't told him that the brakes were almost useless and now the steering wheel was jammed. He had felt that the steering was jammed since we set off, but because the motorway was predominantly straight he hadn't needed any diversion. I tried the steering column and, sure enough, it was jammed in the straight-ahead position. At this point the German owner produced an ignition key and said: "Zat iss to stopp ze theef." We had just encountered our first vehicle with a steering lock fitted.

We forgave ourselves for not realising it had a steering lock because the ignition key was located a long way from the actual column. We both unanimously agreed that this sort of security device would never catch on. It was too complicated and far too dangerous. The poor brakes were the result of servo assist and were missing because the engine was stopped. We also thought this luxury might not catch on either. I think we can now say that on both these matters we would subsequently be proven well and truly wrong.

It was not just foreign cars that started to appear. The motorway seemed to attract foreign lorries, which were nothing short of a nightmare. The drivers either did not or chose not to speak any English, especially if they were in some sort of difficulty. One of the main dilemmas they would find themselves in was that after travelling from Germany through Holland and Belgium and part of France, then arriving by ferry at Dover, they would travel on the relatively flat terrain. This would continue until they reached the North East of England and somehow turned off the motorway. They would then encounter steep gradients and tight corners. It became apparent to us that foreign drivers did not do steep gradients and tight corners, especially if they are uphill. Usually the engine was not powerful enough so the vehicle would become jammed. In these situations all that was needed was for a heavy recovery vehicle to attach a chain and tow the vehicle clear of the hill.

On arrival we would usually ask how heavy the combined lorry and trailer was. We would always be told "38 tons" which at the time was the maximum permitted weight. In fact, the "38 tons" would be repeated over and over again, I assume like a prisoner of war repeating his name, rank and number. The only thing they must have known was that if they had given the true weight, which was probably nearer 50 tons, they would have been locked up by the police with all the difficulties that would bring. I sometimes think if I had asked a driver where he had come from he would say "38 tons" and if I then asked him where he was going to, after we had freed him from the hill, he would once again say "38 tons". To make matters worse, they never seemed to carry any goods that were any use to us, though I did once acquire 2 cwt of onions that kept well over the winter and were absolutely delicious. If the fault was a breakdown we never had any parts because these were well and truly foreign trucks. Usually the vehicle would be sitting about in our compound for the best part of a week while somebody drove from the fatherland with the spare parts. I suppose one thing that amused me was the fact that Walls detested them even more than I did.

However badly we thought they used to cope, it was ten times better than I would have coped if I had had to take something like the Diamond T to France. We hadn't yet entered the world where drivers understood the language fully. This was brought home when one poor unsuspecting French lorry driver pulled into the newly-opened Washington Services and put 300 gallons of petrol in his Diesel tank. He then had no money left for Diesel. He apparently spent the next few days getting the petrol out and selling it cheaper to passing motorists in order to get money for Diesel. This driver was certainly enterprising, if nothing else.

When the new development was sort of completed and opened it was to house a modern Ford main dealership that had little place for a 24-hour breakdown service. Again, we were relocated, this time to a much larger wooden hut in the corner of the site. We felt like German prisoners-of-war. We had a few spare parts, a black and white television and the hut was heated by an old-fashioned night storage heater which was really two or three dozen bricks wrapped in a heater element. These bricks, heated overnight by cheap electricity, were then left to get the place warm during the day, so by 7 o'clock at night we were once again frozen.

To make matters worse, when taking the job originally, my wage was probably two and a half times that of a normal motor mechanic. I was now earning probably 10% or 15% more but was still attending work for a hundred hours each week and we were now approaching the autumn of 1972. A General Manager had been appointed and in his own inimitable style was working his way, week by week, through the various departments cleansing and refreshing. People were waiting with baited breath to see what would happen when he reached the breakdown service. I hadn't had any dealings at all with this individual because he'd normally gone home before I started and, in turn, I was at home before he made his daily appearance. I suppose he was to do me a bigger favour than the rest of the staff put together.

The situation started when I'd towed a Vauxhall VX490 with a broken clutch cable to the workshop. The vehicle was renowned as having the most difficult clutch cable to fit on any car. I wasn't going to attempt this job on a cold October night working outside a wooden hut using a torch. I therefore negotiated with the owner that it would be left for the workshop to repair. The problem was that various messages were never carried and when the customer turned up for his vehicle at 5 o'clock the following night it wasn't done. He complained to this General Manager who elected to stay back and have a word with me. He confronted me when I arrived and asked why I hadn't installed a cable during my shift the previous night. I told him in no uncertain terms that it wasn't my job to fit one last night and I wasn't going to fit one now or ever. He could get his workshop staff to do their job. He then asked me what I'd been doing during the night and I told him that I had felt tired and had gone to sleep in case there were any breakdown jobs to do. He informed me that I shouldn't be working for the company with that sort of attitude and I might as well go home, which is exactly what I did. However, when word got around, Sir telephoned me and persuaded me to continue as I had always done and to ignore this General Manager, which is exactly what I did.

I was approaching the Lombard RAC Rally, which I had entered for the third time as Privateer. However, I had attracted excellent sponsorship and needed to make a good impression. I didn't want this individual distracting me, so I just concentrated on getting everything organised for the rally with the minimum of distraction. Working the long hours and days was starting to become a hindrance to my driving career just as the lack of money had been some 10 years earlier.

It was after completing the event and taking my Third Place in Class that I was having dinner with two other competitors whom I had known for a number of years. The conversation, which was full of bounce and enthusiasm, hinged around their own businesses. Even though they were the same age as me they both had small garage repair workshops and one also had two filling stations. They were going back to enjoy their work and I was going back to work from my wooden hut for a hundred and five hours each week. I also had to put up with the General Manager, not to mention the presence of Walls who, incidentally, this General Manager had assessed and chosen to completely avoid.

So, as I was pouring another cup of coffee and scooping in a spoonful of sugar, I made the momentous decision that I had to start my own business, I had to have a breakdown truck of my own. So, some eight weeks later, just after 8 o'clock one Monday morning in January 1973 I found myself standing outside a workshop in a back street in Durham City as I had done some twelve years earlier in Willington. This time I didn't have to wait for my employer to arrive and knew it was the right time and day because, unlike when I was 15 years old, this workshop was my own: my name was above the door. As I opened the large padlock there were as yet no vehicles inside only a large metal stove that needed to be fired up to get the dampness off the place. As I broke up a wooden pallet, tipped in some petrol and dropped in a match, I realised one thing was for certain, I hadn't lost the knack of lighting a stove and I didn't even singe a single eyebrow.

As I stood over the stove waiting for the place to heat up, the smell of burning coming from the oily metal started to rekindle memories. Since all was quiet, I realised how people and cars had changed so much in only one decade, probably never again would so many changes take place in such a short time. I also reflected how my own life had changed over the previous 20 years. From playing with Dinky cars and experiencing the one-horse power of Jack the farm workhorse to my present situation relating to the workings of real cars and how I'd taken part in three World Championship motor rallies.

Cars had changed very little from the 1920s until the late 50s and suddenly they were now completely different animals, capable of achieving so much more. Just sitting inside the older cars there was a smell of class and comfort, probably combined with foist and rust, something the plastic upholstery and interior of a later vehicle could never provide. A good connoisseur could smell a Singer Vogue a mile away. Just about every other change was for the better. Gone, thank goodness, were the days of six-volt electrics where it was sometimes necessary to get out of the vehicle to see if the headlights were actually working. The modern 12-volt system provided everything. Among other things it propelled a functional heater and electric windscreen washers became a standard fitting.

The old smoky side-valve engine, which enabled a good vehicle to reach almost 60 miles per hour on the downhill, was replaced with engines that would do 100 miles per hour and use only half the fuel in the process. Fortunately everything else kept pace; leaf springs were replaced by independent suspension, cable brakes disappeared in favour of hydraulics and some high performance cars even had disc brakes on the front. Safety features started to appear. Chest piercing steering columns were replaced with padded steering wheels. Ankle straps that had long adorned the door pillars of older cars were replaced with seat belts. Forward opening doors, which often chose to open themselves as the car went over an unsuspected bump, were replaced with doors that hinged on the leading edge, which also featured zero torque safety locks.

More and more vehicles were starting to appear with front wheel drive, something that would not have been considered for mass production, certainly not before the Morris Mini became so successful. Gone were the days when a driver could buy a car in any colour he chose, provided it was a shade of black. Pink, purple and yellow became available and fashionable.

While all this was happening to vehicles, young people seemed to be going in the opposite direction. Disappearing rapidly was the glamour that had started in the 1950s. No longer did a young lad feel that he needed to hit a Saturday night in an expensive suit, tie and winkle pickers: instead scruffy became the image. People would dress down just to go out at night. The saddest part was the demise of the ever so pretty girls, who must have spent hours getting their hair and clothes just right. Gone were high-heeled shoes and, worst of all, gone forever were the glamorous seamed stockings and suspenders, to be replaced by new-fangled equipment called tights, where the latest development appeared to include a reinforced gusset.

I had also broken with tradition as I deserted the red-hot stove and walked over and plugged in a new electric kettle that I had bought the previous Saturday. As I was spreading my tools along the bench I realised that life was about to start a full circle once again. Shortly afterwards I was visited by a Chief Superintendent in charge of Traffic Police in County Durham, who had looked me up to check on a motor sport matter as he was a big supporter. He wandered around the dingy and not yet warm workshop, shook his head in dismay. As he walked out the door to get in his warm patrol car, he said quite decisively and firmly, as he looked me in the eye, "You must have a heart like a lion." He then drove away. Maybe I have.

## Thirty Years On — Where Are They Now?

So, thirty or more years on, it's worth taking a look at where they are now.

Colin Wilson (Wislon): After spending a short while in Dunfermline, Colin moved into motor sport publications, during which time he became a very accomplished co-driver, returning to partner me, winning two British 1600 cc Rally Championships along the way. Colin eventually took an appointment as Communications Manager with the Motor Sport Association (MSA) and became the spokesperson for British Motor Sport for many years before taking an early retirement package and starting his own e-mail communications company. We speak to and see each other frequently and he often stays for Christmas, which ensures that there is no food left over for the dogs!

Alan Able (Sir): Mr. Able is now well retired after selling his successful businesses and living in the manner to which he was always well accustomed. I always remember how much he taught me and how much I learned from him and used in my own business. He was a wonderful inspiration even though I am sure he didn't realise it.

Keith Waters (Bisley): Keith left the motor trade when the company got bigger. It wasn't possible to run the stores from the back of a cigarette packet: certainly not as a Middlesbrough supporter with haemorrhoids. Sadly, he never adapted outside his beloved stores and died tragically a few years later.

Peter Brown (Hovis): Peter has continued as the third or fourth generation of the family engineering business. However, he has downsized considerably and now just controls the very small operation where he enjoys life to the full. We always reminisce and he would not have missed those early days for the world.

George Nichols (GN): After a life of welding and working with steam boilers, George is now retired and trying to fulfil his life's ambition of getting his own steam engine up and running in his backyard. He claims to have made several attempts and almost had it turning, but if he doesn't get it going soon the Council is probably going to put a preservation order on it because it is already that old. (As I write these words someone told me that GN had died suddenly of a heart attack. God bless him.)

John Sharpe (Bisley's Assistant): After a few varied jobs, including many years of driving a Local Authority gritter in the winter months, John has settled into an administrative role looking after supplies at a Local Authority Depot and, like Hovis, he wouldn't have missed those early days and the antics that went with them. But eventually we all grow old.

Lesley Walls (Walls): God knows where he is and, anyway, who cares?

Fred Henderson (The Author): Over 31 years after starting in a dingy back street workshop, the business has expanded to become one of the largest breakdown and recovery services in County Durham and is now known as Breakdown Doctor. The business incorporates a vehicle repair workshop that employs over 20 people, including on work experience the grandson of Alan Bromley. Fred retired from competitive driving in 1984 after being involved with the Toyota and Vauxhall factory teams. In a competitive driving career that spanned almost 20 years and netted two British 1600cc Rally Championships (together with Colin Wilson) he also won over 40 rallies and took part in eleven rounds of the World Rally Championship. At the age of 60 he still plays a game of cricket and drives the odd racing car but the mix of motor sport experience and 40 years of breakdown and recovery work has kept him in demand to recover high value racing cars at many of the country's leading racing circuits. However, the business is run in a 'hands-on' manner and no days will be passed without FH being found under a bonnet with an odd spanner or two. More from www.fredhenderson.com

Barbara May: As a first girlfriend I always remember Barbara. She could be anywhere now, anywhere in the world, or living half a mile away. But I expect wherever she is, she's somebody's Glamorous Gran. In any case I would love to know.

AND FINALLY ......Although I thoroughly enjoyed my work over the years and was very confident in many of the tasks before me, I always felt a bit of a misfit. I always had a slower speech pattern than other people and always tried to choose my words carefully in any form of conversation. I never worried unduly about this but it had been a cause for people to mock me when I was younger. However, I felt exonerated when a girl I particularly liked at school said to her friends that she rather liked the sound of my voice and the way I spoke; that was all I needed to charge me up for the next dozen years. I would become so easily bored with the petty conversation of my fellow workers and their nit picking over some jobs. I was always more concerned with what would happen at the end of the day, and even though I was light years away from it I felt I could identify more easily with people in responsible positions or higher walks of life.

One of my great areas of concern was writing up invoices for jobs that had been done. I would find it so difficult to spell some of the words and would spend five times as long writing out my job sheets as anyone else, using half the words. It would be almost 37 years later when a customer, who was involved in adult literacy, noticed me stumbling to write out a job card and offered to give me a dyslexia test. I have to say that at the time she was hoping I would put myself on one of her courses to improve my literacy. While I was fascinated by what she was telling me I never had any intention of trying to put my learning difficulties right. In fact, I'm not sure I would have wanted to put them right all those years ago. In any case with great enthusiasm I went off to be tested and I have to say how interesting it was, mainly because a whole series of tests had been devised that with my disability would prove a real challenge. I must add that if I hadn't by now overcome my under-confidence I would have come away from the test feeling pretty low. But what sort of test would it have been if I had got all the answers right? When my test results arrived I was deemed to be strongly at risk of being dyslexic. While this diagnosis was not cast in stone, in order to achieve this I would have to go and be certified by a higher body, something like an educational psychologist – modern bureaucracy again! I'd had enough of these tests and in any case it was not going to help me repair cars any better. In fact, being dyslexic was probably an advantage all along.

Since the evaluation I have had a chance to look back at some of my achievements over the past 40 years and I honestly feel I was lucky to suffer from this form of dyslexia. Apart from my writing and spelling, and my lack at mastering some of the less straightforward words in the English language, I do not feel that I have missed out on anything in life. I obviously cannot spell or pronounce any foreign names or places but since I never like them anyhow, that hasn't been a big miss. However, many modern cars have these types of names and yes! I am snookered. There's a lot to be said for Mini or an Imp or a Ford 8, although Polo isn't too bad.

I'm led to believe that the problem may have started when I was 10 years old and I suffered from pleurisy that turned to pneumonia. I finished up in hospital for three weeks with a collapsed lung. When I returned home I was left seriously asthmatic, a condition that remained with me until I was about 15 when it started to subside, allowing me to resume normal physical activities. People used to see me on the farm and more than one person would remark that I was the same colour during an attack as the old Fordson Major tractor that was often parked in the yard. When I look back now it was a horrible shade of blue and I must have looked quite ill. So it's not impossible that my brain was starved of oxygen during the initial illness, leading to this condition. I have now spent many hours looking back and prior to this illness I had no problem keeping up with any subject at school. My failure in English was always put down to the fact that I lost almost a year's schooling. It's funny how that lost year didn't affect any of the other subjects that I was working with and no one noticed this at the time of course.

When reading, I sometimes miss out vital words without realising it, which is not good when trying to follow instructions. So I soon learned that the easiest way to assemble anything was just to take a good look at it and then try and work it out. I have undertaken some fair-sized jobs, including a full sized kitchen and several kits of MFI-type furniture without once studying the instructions.

Many of the things I struggle with and equally many of the things that I'm good at I didn't attribute to dyslexia. The fact that I find it difficult to concentrate if there are external distractions I thought was normal. I found it hard to drive a rally car fast if there was something wrong with it that did nothing else but make a noise, like for example the exhaust dragging on the ground or a piece of bodywork flapping. While this would not in practice slow down the vehicle, I would find it very hard to concentrate. On more than one occasion I finished up going off the road through this type of distraction. Like all other problems associated with this condition I found my own solution. I therefore always wore a good quality, good fitting crash helmet with the intercom linked only to the co-driver, thereby drowning out all background noise. It is interesting that at no point did the co-driver calling out instructions relating to the road ahead distract me.

It is dyslexia that stops me from doing two things at once, but I can certainly oversee several subjects at any one time by spending five minutes on each one and then going on to the next one, and so on then back to the first without losing the plot.

These few things fade into insignificance at least in a lifetime when I consider some of the gifts I've been given. I have never needed a tape measure to put a picture up straight; I once erected a whole 30 metre fence and never measured a paling. Perhaps my greatest gift is my ability to assess an overall situation, calculating any risk and be able to see the end result more clearly than most people. Unfortunately, this makes dealing with people harder. I now find that I need to be more tolerant because most people do not have the transparency to see what I can see. But even after understanding these things I still find myself hopelessly intolerant of people with small minds. Certainly when I was at school, but even over the intervening years I am perceived by many people as being a bit 'thick', especially when they considered my slow speech. This was very hurtful and took quite a long time to come to terms with, but now if anybody thinks that, they should be warned they do so at their own risk! Because one thing is for sure, if that is what they think, who am I to make them any wiser?

Dyslexia can apparently cause short-term memory problems. Again, using hindsight, I have often found it difficult when connecting wiring looms to remember which wire is which. I can check a certain colour at the tail-light and by the time I get back round to the bonnet I have forgotten which colour it is. But once again I thought everyone was like that. There is another area I have always had a problem with and now I know why. Ever since I started my own business I've had to put up notices giving staff instructions. After putting a notice up, some two months later I would spot that a couple of words were round the wrong way. No one had dared say anything and in any case the longer-term staff just got used to it. But since I've been diagnosed I now get someone else to print the notices, just in case.

I believe another phenomenon I have taught myself is to know when to top up my sleep. I can consciously decide to take 15 or 20 minutes shut-eye, going into such a deep slumber that as I wake I forget where I am. Yet after no more than five seconds I am restored to full mental faculties and fully refreshed for at least another three hours. This ability served me well during some of the long international rallies that I took part in but is still useful when carrying out long distance relays. While other people will try to freshen themselves with black coffees, etc., I will simply take one of my sleep breaks which are much better than anything that comes out of a cup.

The condition is reputed to give very good spatial awareness and I certainly have been able to drive a Rally car as well as anyone in the country. I could extend this ability to anything mechanical whether it is a piece of farm machinery or a piece of earth moving equipment like a JCB. While all of these observations are based on hindsight, I am very conscious that my particular type of dyslexia has been better for me in many ways; not everyone is that lucky. Some dyslexia is a real disability but I now say to people who ask me about this condition: "Just get on and do what you are good at and if you find just one area that you excel in, it does your confidence a world of good."

**Other books in the series:**

**CAB 1 Tales from the life of a York taxi driver.**
**By Peter Birchenall**

**ISBN 0-9548056-0-7**
**Price £5.95**

Over 26 years York taxi driver Tony Baker took an untold number of people to hundreds of different destinations. Each journey was different. He became a counsellor, adviser and friend to many people. He was subject to violence, threats of violence and amorous advances, with each situation demanding a tactful approach that can only come from experience. Tony's work included the transportation of non-human cargo including cats, chickens and furniture, sometimes to destinations high in the North Yorkshire Moors, often with unpredictable consequences.

**MORE THAN I DESERVED.**
**By Rosie Shannon**

**ISBN 0-9548056-1-5**
**Price £6.50**

Rosie Shannon is the daughter of a Nottinghamshire farm worker. She lives in the market town of Retford. In her life she has experienced marital break up, serious illness and the sudden death of a child; she has fought against the terrible effects of physical and sexual abuse, yet somehow survived. A life split into two halves by love and hate, both experienced by the same woman. Rosie Shannon's account of her life is testimony to a courageous woman, she is a fighter and her story will give hope to other women who find that, for them, life is less than fair.

These books can be obtained from Reading Room Publishing, 45 Forest Road, Warsop, Mansfield, Nottinghamshire, NG20 0ER. Please add £1.50 per book to cover postage and packaging.